Each Time She Wakes
Sophia

Katy Tackes

inSpīrus8™ Publishing

Laguna Niguel, CA

This work is dedicated to my husband, for his strength of character, his unwavering support and his steadfast love.

Acknowledgement

To my beloved distant sage, Helena P. Blavatsky; for it is by her gracious act of unveiling the Light that my Sophia awakes.

"Wisdom begins in wonder."

— SOCRATES

CHAPTER ONE

She awakens to find a silken thread draped across her lap. Smiling, she lifts the creation up to the rising sun. On one end of the thread hangs a strand of pearls, on the other, a golden needle.

The sun's ray arouses the needle's attention. It's time to choose the next pearl she thinks. Gently laying the strand down on an ocean of midnight-blue velvet, she looks over the sea of loose pearls sprinkled before her. Each one is unique; each an individual testimony to the beauty of Nature.

Viewing her options, she recognizes the frail ones, bold ones, "perfect" ones; some with imperfections right out front, others with their flaws hidden deep within.

She leans back again to focus her guiding Light. From a far corner, one pink little pearl rolls into sight, reflecting its full potential. Just then a bright ray of sunshine glistens onto the point of the golden needle. Swooping up this tiny pearl, she pierces it as it sparkles its way onto the beautiful strand.

"Your journey has begun my little darling," she whispers, with a deep sense of love for her newest creation.

CHAPTER TWO

The beads of sweat enter with a burning sting as they roll into Roger Cahill's eyes. He is sprinting across the parking lot, at Palamo Regional Hospital to reach his beloved wife before she gives birth. The hospital doors silently sweep open as he nears the entrance. Between breathless pants, he spurts out, "Hope Cahill...she's having our baby...Where is she...Can I see her?"

The attendant at the reception desk calms Roger down, and directs him to the maternity waiting room on the 5th floor. Off he goes, excited, anxious, full of adoration and affection for his one true love who is about to give him the most precious gift.

CHAPTER THREE

"It's a girl!" declares the nurse, while working quickly to clear the baby's airways, document her birth stats and bundle her up for the newest mom at Palamo Regional Hospital.

Hope Cahill endured a hard labor of love to deliver the 7 pound, 4 ounce angel. The nurse lays the little pink bundle onto Hope's chest.

"You are my miracle baby," her mother thinks aloud. "My little darling, you are truly a gift to us," she whispers to her swaddled newborn while gently kissing her forehead. "Where is Roger? I want my husband here with us to rejoice in our little creation. It's all so perfect now," Hope whispers with her last breath. As the lights brighten before her, Hope fades away.

"Hope, Hope!!" yells the head maternity nurse as she snatches the baby from Hope's lifeless arms. The chaos is getting louder as the doctor and nurses begin their dance of revival. It is no use. Hope has suffered a sudden death brain aneurysm.

Young Sophia Grace Cahill begins her life's journey during the very moments that her mother ends hers.

CHAPTER FOUR

Roger runs into the waiting room, he approaches the nurse on duty, asking for Hope. The nurse is fully aware of the terrible news that Roger Cahill is about to receive. She cautiously tells him, "Mr. Cahill, won't you please take a seat, and someone will be with you shortly." Then she asks, "Um, Mr. Cahill, is anyone else here with you?" Sitting on the edge of the seat, he shakes his head 'no', as a cold shudder shoots down his spine.

The hospital doors sweep open for Hope's doctor. He walks slowly toward Roger. He is fiddling with his clipboard, looking nervously above Roger's head, as if he is searching for something.

Roger leaps up asking, "How is she, Doctor? How is my wife? Can I see our baby?" With each question, the doctor's eyes sink lower. Roger feels the cold surrounding him again. "What is it? Tell me. I've been sitting here waiting to go in. Christ, just tell me what is going on!"

As if reading from a checklist, the doctor responds, "Mr. Cahill, please calm down, take a seat. You have a very healthy, strong and beautiful baby girl...but, I'm sorry...Your wife suffered a sudden death brain aneurysm. It was instant…"

The rest of his words are drowned out by the noise and chaos within Roger's mind. He falls to the floor. The weight of the words, are crushing him. He can feel the whole world closing in on him. All Light seems to disappear in that one moment.

Then he hears the faint calling of Hope's voice, "I will be with you always. Look for me. You are not alone. You have our little darling…you have Sophia."

As her voice warms his heart, a soft glow takes over his sight. He feels warmth surrounding him again. "Light is near…" Roger hears with a distinct tone that catches his attention.

Once again he can hear the doctor, "Would you like to see your daughter?"

Roger is lifted up and led toward the room where Sophia and Hope shared two very different outcomes of the same event. He cannot bear to look forward, his head bobbles with each step. The squeaking of his shoes against the linoleum sets a comforting rhythm. His mind clings onto the sound immediately; anything to drown out the fear of his own thoughts. Then his sight catches the subtle swish of chiffon fabric flowing in and out of sight with each step. Roger follows the swaying movement with his eyes until he hears a soft, deep voice whispering, "We will overcome this, Mr. Cahill. You are not alone."

The whispers come from a rotund lady walking alongside Roger with her arm around him, almost holding him up. Her dark, tear-covered cheeks cradle a reassuring smile as she continues whispering, "We will overcome this. I will not leave your side till the strength of your will matches the strength of your love for that new little girl. Oh no sir, you will not be alone."

Roger hears Hope's voice again, telling him, "Hold tight to this woman, she is your guiding light now." When he hears those words, he can smell Hope's perfume as if she is standing right beside him.

They stop at the door leading to Hope. Roger peers through the small window panel to where his beautiful wife rests, as though she is sleeping. The doctor interrupts the silence, "Mr. Cahill, would you like to have a moment with Hope? You can go in...if that's what you want."

"No, no, I can't. I don't..." Roger is stumbling over his words and emotions.

Just then, the woman holding him up eases in toward Roger and shares, "Mr. Cahill, go on in. It's important for you, but even more important for her. You need to set her soul free from the beautiful vessel that holds it here on Earth. Go on Mr. Cahill, open your heart to hers." Somehow when this woman speaks, Roger trusts her. He can sense that she is here to guide him through this turmoil, like a beacon of light.

The bond of trust gets its first affirmation as Roger takes a step closer to the entrance. The weight of the door is immense but Roger pushes forward. The room is eerily quiet. Now, the squeaking of his shoes is almost funny...like the punch-line to a bad joke.

Reaching her side, Roger takes Hope's hand in both of his and clutches her to his heart. The thoughts ebb and flow as if they are waves in an ocean of images. His emotions rise and fall. When his sobbing interrupts their communion, warmth encircles Roger and brings an awkward but loving smile to his face. Thousands of images are flashing before them; the wonders they have experienced together. Every moment that made an impression is being released once more--from the silliness of their first date, when Hope laughed suddenly, snorting chocolate shake through her perfect little nose...to Hope being the rock of support while Roger gave the heart-wrenching eulogy at the passing of his dear mother just a few months ago.

Roger tearfully says good-bye to Hope, letting go of her hand. The circle of warmth wanes, but Roger senses he will always have Hope.

CHAPTER FIVE

There is a bounty of colorful flowers, lovingly placed around one majestic old oak. Folks from the island are crowding onto Great Oak's Knoll, for the services. That sole oak tree is smack dab in the heart of the forty-acre parcel of land that Roger and Hope inherited just a few months ago.

The land had been gifted to Roger's grandfather by the local tribal council. It was for his great achievement in engineering. Roger's grandfather had built a small dam, during a rare season of drought. This allowed the meager mountain run-off to create a pool of crystal clear water for their tribe to survive the drought and eventually thrive over the years. In return for his actions, the council granted to Roger's grandfather a portion of this sacred land, by way of these forty acres. Up until just a few days ago, this land was to be the site of Hope and Roger's dream home--the one they had planned and designed together over the last few years.

Today the land is getting renamed 'Hope's Haven' as her favorite oak tree is welcoming her home one final time. It is a beautiful service, with many of her friends and relatives sharing their stories of remembrance.

Roger sits in disbelief at the events of the past several days. His heart is broken, as if it were a shattered vase. As people continue their fond memories, Roger's thoughts begin to get louder; pounding through his head. "How could this happen to us? Why would you leave me...Leave us? What am I to do with a baby? Alone, how can I? What will this baby think? Who am I to raise this child? Help me, Hope...help me." With each thought, life expels from his body. He works to remind himself to breathe in, time and again.

When he sees any glimmer of Hope, despair quickly tramples over their love....grief morphs into loneliness...loneliness sinks into fear. It takes time for Roger to crawl out of this depth, but time brings about change.

Slowly, the seasons change. Summer blurs into autumn, autumn wanes into winter, winter begrudgingly releases its hold on spring.

Roger spends many evenings walking up to that mighty oak atop Hope's Haven. The breeze kisses the back of his neck each time, as he sits on the bench he had built for their nightly visits. As the breeze lifts his spirits, he thinks about his beautiful wife. He remembers how she would wake him up each morning with a gentle kiss on the back of his neck.

There is sense of peace under the oak, where Roger confides in Hope. This is where he feels her love the most. He hears her on the breeze. He feels her; he is not alone...just as she had promised. With each visit, Roger claims the moment with the same thought, "It's so peaceful, here." Peace--the sound of his fears surrendering to her love.

It has been a few long years since Hope has left him. Three years since Roger's heart had been filled to the brim with the anticipation of his beautiful daughter then shattered into a million little pieces with the death of his wife. Yet, every day since, he picks up another piece and slowly reconstructs his broken heart. One filled with love for his daughter, but inevitably full of deep cracks over the loss of Hope. His intuition often tells him, "Those cracks are there to allow Hope's memories to pass through freely". But the memories cannot make him whole. His shattered heart will need a miracle in order to heal.

CHAPTER SIX

"Oh my, she is growing up so fast," proclaims Astar, the caregiver Roger Cahill hired to calm the frenzy that had so suddenly become part of his daily life. "Sophia, come on inside now, honey. It's almost time for dinner."

Sophia is bent over a rock, cupping a robin that is injured. The bird barely fits onto the three-year-old, little girl's hand. She lays her right hand on the robin's frail wing, rubbing it gently as she whispers something to it.

Astar shows Roger through the kitchen window and tells him, "She's helping that little ole robin. Her wing is broken for sure…but Sophia is spreading her love…yes, sir, our little girl is spreading her love."

Just then Sophia releases the robin. It flies onto her shoulder and nuzzles her cheek before flying off into the woods.

Roger watches his daughter in wonder and disbelief at what he has just witnessed. He can feel his heart grow at the sight of this miracle.

Yet, Astar feels this is just another day in young Sophia's life. "She's building her treasure chest of wisdom," Astar quietly whispers to herself, knowingly.

Astar is great for the Cahills. She is a larger-than-life, bright soul, who takes care of them both as though this is her one mission in life. Her energetic, lively and animated demeanor is a daily blessing. She has a knack for giving love, in every moment of the day. No matter what your ailment, Astar can fix it with a kind word, a love-filled embrace, or a mystical story. Her love, like sunshine, warms your soul.

While watching Sophia respond to Astar, Roger reflects on the night Astar came into their lives. She was in the hospital on the day Sophia was born. It was a blessing she was there.

Astar was the woman in the maternity waiting room when Roger had received the devastating news. She witnessed his anguish, and was drawn to his needs. She had wrapped her arms around him, and kept telling him, "You are not alone; you have your little darling baby. I am here for you. I won't let you walk through this darkness alone."

From that first time he met this lovely lady in flowing chiffon, till this very moment, Astar has been by Roger's side. He believes Hope had a hand in Astar coming into their lives. Just as she promised, Hope's words continue to linger with Roger, 'You are not alone'.

Yes, Astar has been good for them all, her *and* her powerful intuition. Her visions continuously protect this little family, and keep everything on track, as though she has access to a master plan. She is their guiding star, shining brightly in their lives, and helping to guide Sophia's journey along the way.

CHAPTER SEVEN

The years keep falling away like the autumn leaves as Sophia grows her treasures and skills. Sophia likes to play in the garden where Hope used to tend to the flowers in her leisure time. Sometimes Hope enters Sophia's secret thought garden, planting seeds of love and creating memories out of imaginary moments.

Sophia practices preparing a special serving of 'grass tea' and 'mud pie' for her honored guest. They laugh and sing along with all the curious woodland creatures that timidly make their way into her circle of friends. They too can sense the spirit of Hope around them.

Sophia feels her mother's love on the warm summer breeze as it caresses her flowing hair and gently places a kiss on her forehead each time. Often, her father feels Hope's presence too. It is magical when he comes out and joins them for a 'spot of tea'. These are the moments they share together. Sophia knows she is never alone on her path. A path that is becoming clearer to her as each year passes.

Roger encourages Sophia to be strong, independent and curious about the wonders of Nature, letting her discover the mysteries of Hope's Haven to her heart's content. He shares stories of Hope's love of Nature and how they can be closest to her when they are in the wilderness.

Over the years, Sophia's love and connection with Nature grows deeply, nurtured by both her parents. She spends her days exploring the beauty of Hope's Haven, in order to discover the magic within herself. Something is brewing deep within her. She senses it. What used to be angels in her dreams are becoming daytime visions in the woods. Nature speaks to her, and Sophia listens well.

This land is Sophia's little piece of heaven. She is growing up here, witnessing nature's cycle of life: creation, growth and dissolution, only to be reborn again. She peeks upon robins' eggs coming to life, meadow flowers bursting to greet the morning sun, tadpoles evolving to become the mighty croakers of the pond, breaking the silence of the evening. These are the colors of her life's palette. Over the past seven years, Sophia has blended Nature's mist into her personal daily mural.

On this day, during one of her adventure hikes, Sophia comes upon the lifeless body of a timber wolf. It is bleeding from its chest. The wound is fresh. The blood trails upon the earth are slowly taking form. Sophia must act quickly to ensure this life is not lost before its sacred time.

This scared young girl approaches the wolf cautiously. She now sees it has been shot. Sophia's anger can only be controlled by her desire to heal this beautiful beast of Nature. As she gets even closer the whimper of the wolf becomes audible. They connect eyes before Sophia feels it is safe to get any closer. There is a thread of trust between the two of them. Sophia leans over the wolf. Ever so gently, she cleans out the wound then lays her hand over the area. She whispers something into the wolf's heart, with that the wolf feebly stands on all fours. He slowly gains his strength as Sophia continues to hold her right hand over the wound. The wolf never breaks his eye contact with her. Amazingly she heals his shattered heart with the power of love flowing through her young self.

Once the timber wolf regains much of his strength, he eases up close to Sophia till they are almost nose to nose. He nuzzles her head in gratitude then makes his way back into the woods.

"Sophia's skills are growing with her bravery," affirms Astar, as she acknowledges the powerful vision she receives from the nearby woods. "Roger, you know she's a very special girl. You know there will come a time when her skills will need to be developed beyond what I can do here. Sophia must spread her wings in order to realize her potential, one day."

Roger supportively begins, "Astar, you are doing a tremendous job home-schooling her. She's doing great in all her subjects." But as he realizes where Astar is heading with this discussion, his irritation becomes noticeable. "I don't see why we need to get the others involved in her education right now, not yet, it's too soon!" Roger's heightened awareness make his words jump out with a sharp edge.

"Roger, you know that's not exactly what I meant..."

"Yes, Astar, unfortunately, I know *exactly* what you mean. I'm just not ready to accept this inexorable truth. She will have to wait....*they* will have to wait...but, I know the time is coming soon enough." Roger's acquiescence becomes apparent in his vulnerable tone. He understands what the future holds, and he knows his rebellion would fall upon deaf ears, when the time comes.

Sophia enters the kitchen and runs to her father's open arms. Breathless from her enthusiastic pace, she gulps for air as she begins to unfold the details behind Astar's vision. Sophia explains how she saved a great timber wolf from bleeding to death in the woods while she embraces the courage she feels for having done it. This courage will become her best friend over the years to come.

Sophia is something special, alright. Roger knows it, Astar knows it…and slowly others will come to understand. For now, Roger is happy to have her close to him. Sophia's daily adventures preoccupy his days while the memory of Hope fills his nights.

Sophia's curious nature does not stop at sundown though; each summer night, after dinner, Sophia runs upstairs to climb out the dormer window of her bedroom and lay on the rooftop. On clear nights, as dusk wanders into the deep blue sky, slowly revealing its hidden treasures, Sophia finds her way to the cosmos. Here she connects with her mother's spirit while watching Hope dancing amongst the stars. Tonight, she shares her wonderful healing story with her mom on that rooftop. As her words turn into the sweetest dreams, Sophia melts away into the midnight-blue velveteen sky, feeling the warm breeze caress her to sleep.

Time keeps moving forward. She will be leaving Hope's Haven, in due time. For now, she still has a few more summers to linger in her favorite spot on Earth.

CHAPTER EIGHT

Roger nervously chokes back his tears as he confesses to Astar, "I have always known that she will not be mine to keep. I have been struggling with the knowledge that Sophia is a gift, not just for me, but for us, all of us. I have to let her go, right?" Roger looks up at Astar wondering if she has a way of changing the inevitable.

Astar sends a nod toward Roger, affirming that once he gave his word so many years ago, destiny began to pave the journey for them all.

"Oh what have I done Astar? I knew this time would come, when I would have to part with her. It's just so damn difficult. She is my darling little girl, and always will be. Why am I put in this position, again? Why do I have to let go of someone I love so dearly? Why do I have to allow my heart to shatter again?"

As soon as Roger asks these selfish questions, the answers come through him with crystal clarity as he states with resignation, "I know, it is only by releasing her that Sophia will be able to learn more and do more. She will seek the truth in order to reach her full potential. I believe in her." He sighs deeply, "I've always known this day would come."

Once more, under his breath, his selfish ego whispers, "I just never knew how painful it would be to have to release yet another soul I love."

When Roger's pain feels over-whelming, he gets a sense of moving out of his body, like he is floating just a few feet above, observing his own life. He is being guided by a spirit or Light. He is filled with warmth, calmness and contentment. While he's not sure how or why it happens, he is grateful when it does.

Over the past several months, as the foreseeable day of Sophia's departure is drawing closer, Roger repeatedly feels the tugging between his selfish ego--that of a father wanting more time with his daughter--and the spirit that so often brings him peace, love and guidance.

CHAPTER NINE

Today is a very special day. Sophia has come of age. It is her twelfth birthday. Birthdays, in the Cahill household, are a little different than most. On your day of birth, you are the one who gives gifts to the ones you love. The sense of giving, being so much more gratifying than receiving, is profoundly felt in this home. It is a family tradition that they have shared as long as Sophia can remember. This year, she has a special gift to share, but not until the time is right.

Sophia quickly packs the last of her things, makes her bed and throws on her favorite sweater. It belonged to her mother. Hope used to wear this sweater every weekend when tending to her flower garden. Even though the years have not been too kind to the sweater, Sophia still feels like she's getting a big hug from Mom every time she wears it. She stops at the mirror to give the memory of her mother a smile and a wink, but their connection is interrupted by the hooting and hollering that is getting louder from down in the kitchen. She eagerly runs down the stairs to get in on the excitement.

Astar and Roger both cheer, "Happy Birthday!" as Sophia runs into the kitchen.

"Let's have it Birthday Girl. Where are the surprises? What little trinkets have you picked up for us this year?" Roger chuckles, as he beckons for his gift from his young daughter. Astar can see through the cajoling to his tear-filled eyes and heavy heart. She walks over to Roger and softly lays a comforting hand on his shoulder.

Sophia is now bubbling over with anticipation as she chimes in, "Not quite yet Daddy, you will have to wait for your gifts. I've got all my things ready to go, but first, I need you to do something for me, one more time. I need you to tell us the story of your vision--the amazing one in the Rocky Mountains."

Sophia pulls out a kitchen chair for Astar as she gestures for her to take a seat. "Astar, you've got to hear this the way Daddy tells it. Oh, and it's an important part of your gifts, so...everyone, pay attention." She smiles teasingly then takes a seat close to her dad.

The truth is that Astar has heard this story many times. Heck, she probably is in on it based on the strength of her intuition. Regardless, the magic and wonder of this incredible story warms Roger's heart, although now they have progressed much farther along in his fateful vision. He is aware that his time with Sophia is diminishing quickly.

As Roger begins, he feels the power of an electric energy swirling around him as it fills his thoughts. The mystic memory slowly emerges from his lips as his voice expresses the inspiring vision, "My darling little girl, *my Sophia*. You have blossomed into quite a beautiful, young lady. You're a kind-hearted soul that has been a gift to us...even before the day you were born.

"When we were young, your mother and I had quite the life--parties, traveling from one destination to another, visiting with all the other young couples trying to get ahead in this world. We were on a mission to amass wealth, homes, cars, jewels, friends, and even memories. You name it, we had to have it. All we did was work hard and play even harder. One depleted our minds and the other depleted our bodies. The worst part was that no matter how much we had, or how much we accomplished, there was emptiness deep within us both. Many times we discussed having children but amidst our busy schedules, we never stopped to plan for any."

Roger enters the vision once again as the images come alive through his words, "One summer, many years ago, while camping in the Rockies, something very special happens deep within your mother's heart. After a long hike, your mother stops to rest." Roger glances up for just a moment, as if acknowledging Hope's memory before continuing.

"While she is lying back on a large granite stone, she begins to ponder her life...thoughts of motherhood flicker about. She is contemplating if the ability and desire to have a child is passing her by. She has so many questions. Can she give up her career? Will she loose her figure? Is it the right time? She thinks to herself that there are so many arguments against bringing a child under her care. She then takes a deep breath and asks her guiding spirit for a sign, some direction....anything!

"Just then the clouds form into a perfect little, infant-shaped poof. The message is clearly displayed in the wispy cloud...so clear, that it brings your mother to tears, then laughter, and afterwards she wonders if she is just light-headed from the hike or the altitude. That same night, when Mom shares her vision with me, we laugh about it over dinner at the campfire."

Roger leans forward in his chair, looking at Astar and Sophia. Then with marvel in his voice he goes on, "But the funny thing is that we--your mother and I--we can feel the magic around us. There is electricity in the air that we both can sense. It lingers with us throughout the night, even as we lounge in our sleeping bags and gaze up at the stars."

He sits back again pondering the memory, "That evening, we both realize that something has changed for us, but we are not sure what, how, or even why."

He slows his voice and lifts the index finger of his right hand, "We had to be patient, in order for the wisdom to come.

"So, exactly one year later, we go back to the same place in the Rockies. I find another magnificent view. This one is perched high on a grassy knoll, over-looking a meadow, with the Bow River down below and massive granite mountains rising high above. As I'm sitting there, I begin to feel myself melting into this scene and becoming one with it, like the brush stroke of a master painter."

Roger begins to feel his own aura brighten as he relives the mystic wonder of his vision. "I am sitting in utter gratitude of this moment in time. I remember that I am fully present yet it feels like I am a purer version of myself. All the demands of life have been lifted, and I feel completely unburdened. I begin repeating aloud, my gratitude and praise, as a swell of exuberance and power fills my body. My entire being is swimming in wonder, gratitude, trust, and *that's* when it happens. In a flash of immense clarity I receive a golden truth so commanding that it changes who I am, forever. This wisdom encompasses me with a depth and breadth of love that words alone cannot express. This love comes at me, through me, around me. I have multiple visions of the future, in vivid colors and exquisite details. I have instantly become aware, but I have no idea of how this knowledge is crystallizing into pure *wisdom* nor do I know the source. The energy and electricity ripples through my body. It is during this time that I envision a beautiful baby girl coming to us or rather through us."

Roger caresses Sophia's check, "Hmm, the message was as clear then, as it is now.

"That night, your mother and I were enlightened that a child will be gifted to us. This child will encompass the wisdom and purity that had just been awakened within us. But, the child will come with a tremendous responsibility. It will be our choice to accept the invitation, or not.

"Your mom and I both sensed there was only one choice for us. A spark of light had ignited within our souls. That spark will go on to light many candles along its path. Our calling is to not stand in its way. Once we made up our minds, our lives would never be the same again.

"When we knew you were on your way, we thought hard to find a name to fit this perfect gift of wisdom we were about to receive. It didn't take long before 'Sophia' came to us."

Roger stops abruptly in order to hold back his tears. He embraces his daughter with a warm bear hug, wanting to never let her go.

"I love asking you to tell me this story, Dad. Each time I feel like I learn a little more, and become even closer to you and Mom. I love you all so very much," whispers Sophia, while hugging Roger, Astar and the spirit of Hope.

"I know sweetheart, now where's my shiny new birthday gift? Where did you hide it, I've been poking around and asking Astar, but no signs of it yet, kiddo." Roger keeps coaxing just to keep his tears at bay.

"Not yet, Dad. I've got everything packed. Are you ready to go up?" Sophia asks with her signature smile and curious energy.

"I'm ready darlin', let's go." Roger has many things to share with Hope this visit, as Sophia is making her last preparations before leaving Hope's Haven. He is going to need Hope more than ever now.

A musty-scented breeze hints at the approaching rain, as they head out to the trailhead. The air becomes cold and heavy with moisture, but the clouds are not yet ready to part with their creation.

The path toward the heart of Hope's Haven is well worn. Her loved ones have made their way up the path to their private bench under that mighty oak many times. At this cherished place they share another tradition that has come about as a healing process introduced by Astar. They often share a part of themselves, weaving special moments with Hope's memory, under that big old oak. They connect their individual stories with the spirit of Hope, bringing them all closer together.

It's a long winding path, around the meadow and up onto the highest bluff on the property. The hill is usually sun-drenched, even when the valley below may be hidden in a blanket of fog.

They begin at the trailhead, making their way up until they come to the first fork in the path. Suddenly, Roger stops. "Hey, what's this?" he asks as he curiously touches the newfound, hand-made marker. He runs his fingers along the symbol, following the burnished curves of the wooden letter "S" until his fingers meet with a small, rough-cut letter "i" that appears to be laid in gold.

Roger gently taps his forehead as if to trigger a memory. This symbol is one he recognizes from his vision, but he can't quite place it. Curiously, when he touches the symbol again, it is warm beneath his fingers. He lingers on the "S" then moves the tip of his finger slowly over the "i". Oddly, the "i" is very cold. Roger is perplexed at the two temperatures and wonders out loud, "Sophia, where did you get this?"

"I can't tell you, not yet...we have to keep going, now hurry before it starts pouring rain." Sophia coyly persuades her father, as they continue their hike along the right fork of the path, around the meadow, to the base of the next hill where another symbol appears, marking the way up the bluff:

Roger's eyes widen when he sees the second symbol. "Ok, this one looks familiar too. It's coming to me, a little. Sophia, I've seen these before, but I can't recall much about them. How did you get these?" He definitely remembers the second symbol emerging from his vision many years ago, but he still can't quite make out its context.

Intrigued, Roger is wondering what his daughter is up to. How does she know about these symbols? He has never described the images to anyone. Does she understand what the symbols mean? Will she reveal it, so *he* can understand what they mean? His desire for answers keeps growing.

He reaches over to touch the second symbol as his fingertips gauge the temperature of the two letters. The "S" and the lower case "i" are now joined together forming a stylized figure-8. Both letters feel the same, but both are warm, unusually warm.

Roger wonders if Astar has helped to create these symbols, "Did Astar put you up to this? Is this one of her science projects?" But Sophia intently keeps walking, with no response to her father's questions. Roger hurriedly tries to catch up to her.

Upon reaching their destination, Roger is surrounded by that once familiar energy that had filled his senses with wonder, in the Rocky Mountains. As he nears the giant oak, he sees the third and final symbol, ∞ hanging by a thick gold-toned chain that has been wrapped around its hearty trunk.

Roger is overcome with emotion as he gently places the bouquet of flowers, they had picked from their garden, beneath the symbol. He appreciates the significance of the infinity shape and is touched by his daughter's acknowledgement of this special place.

As he approaches the beautiful carving the symbol begins to glow and exude gentle warmth. Roger moves in closer to it. He reaches out to touch the symbol. It captures a ray of light and sends it toward Roger, almost playfully teasing him. He's startled. "Wow, is the sun doing that?" Again the symbol's familiar energy draws him near. His fingers inquisitively trace the full glory of the infinity sign. Every hair on his body rises up as the energy fills Roger with uplifting emotion. His memory rushes back once again to his sacred vision of years past. As Roger's hand graces the symbol another time, he turns and reaches for his daughter with his free hand. He hugs her in a powerful embrace. "Sophia, honey, how did you do this? What do you know about these symbols? Can you tell me more about them? I have seen these symbols before, they must mean something, but I can't say that I know or understand anything about them."

"Dad, all I know is that they've been coming to me in my dreams, and showing me these three symbols. Over the years the symbols have become clearer to me, yet I don't know what they mean, either. They told me to finish these symbols by my twelfth birthday. They showed me where to harvest the wood and how to shape the letters. The gold on the 'i' came from a crumbled stone I found near this special wood. I think they look fantastic, don't you Daddy?"

"They are fantastic sweetheart." Roger takes a deep breath, and begins to spark a fire in the stone ring he had built nearby. As the fire takes hold, they both settle in around the flames. Once again Roger feels the soft caress of the breeze on the back of his neck, letting him know Hope is nearby. "I think your mother is interested in hearing what this is all about, too." He says under his breath.

"Sophia honey, come here and sit down. Can you fill in some more details for me? Like, *who exactly* has been coming to you in your dreams? What are these people telling you? What else have you seen in your dreams?" Roger becomes anxious, he is concerned for Sophia but he also wants to hear what she may have discovered.

Sophia smiles, "Dad, I hope you're ready to hear this. You might think some of what I'm about to say is a little unbelievable, but you have to know, deep down, it's all true.

You will have to believe me when I tell you, I've seen it. I've seen your vision, the one you had in the wilderness. Portions of it have been coming to me in my dreams since I can remember, but now I see it vividly in my waking hours. I just have to focus on it, and there it is." Sophia gently clutches her father's hand in hers and holds it close to her heart.

"Dad, I understand what is expected of me. I've seen the visions, even the parts you have tried so hard to keep to yourself. It's OK, Dad. I will be fine. Please don't worry. They have been guiding me since I was three years old, at least. I know it is my time to go. I've been having visions and dreams about this journey all my life, and these three symbols are part of this adventure, I know it. Maybe they are clues to my future path. I don't know for sure, but I am ready to find out. I'm not afraid, Daddy. Remember, I have that spirit of love with me, the one you and mom share."

To stop herself from tearing up she slowly pats the dirt into a smooth drawing surface then, using a stray eagle feather, she traces out one of the symbols:

"This first symbol has been in my memory the longest. I remember being in my crib and dreaming of Mom singing to me as this symbol would sway from side to side into view. I always thought this was how Mom would connect with me. I'd see the two letters--the 'S' and that little 'i'--always connected at the top, yet free-flowing down below. It was like the two letters were in a dance. I would reach for this symbol all the time as it hovered all around my crib. It would playfully coax me to chase it. I think this is what got me walking so early, remember? And getting me into trouble too, huh?" Sophia jokes with her dad. "But Dad, there's more, so much more." Sophia becomes serious again, as she begins drawing the figure-8 symbol.

8 "The second symbol began coming to me after I saved the wolf. Remember my timber wolf, Dad? The first time I saw this figure-8 symbol was in the trails of blood left behind by him. The blood formed a perfect 8--so perfect I just had to touch it. When I put my fingers into the warmth of his blood, I felt an incredible connection to Nature, an understanding that we are all a part of it. We are all connected."

Sophia fondly remembers the wolf, "My timber wolf was an awesome creature. Oh how I wish I could see him again. He and I bonded that day." She looks up at her father as her face expresses the strength of that bond. "There is a sense of trust and love between us that is about as strong as yours and mine Dad."

Sophia twirls the feather along her cheek to stop herself from tearing up then she uses it, once again, to draw the last symbol into the soft dirt. "The third symbol, ∞ started making itself known last month, right around the time they revealed to me that my path will lead me far away from home for now. This symbol always comes to me on warm, white light and hovers right above my head. When it is near, I feel powerful and a part of something bigger than I could ever imagine.

"I don't have any answers, just a lot of questions. But, Dad, I want you to know that we are always connected--you and I--we are never alone....my love will always be with you...and yours with me, no matter where we are. *This* I know."

Her words leave Roger speechless. All he can do is embrace his daughter and keep this moment for his memories, for he thinks this may be the last sunset they will ever witness together...

CHAPTER TEN

Night has fallen quickly upon this mid-September day. Back at the house, Roger quietly enters Sophia's bedroom and sits alongside her bed. His young daughter left quite an impression on his heart with the sharing of her gifts and visions today.

He gently sweeps back her hair as he watches her eyelids slowly sink into slumber. "Goodnight my sweet darling. Tomorrow you will begin the next part of your journey."

Roger can feel the burden of worry once again. In his mind he begins his lamentations, "My heart aches at having to let you go. Your mother and I have always known this day would come. You were never ours to keep. You are a free spirit…always have been.

"Your gifts are to be cultivated now, and shared with the world. Just promise me, that I will see you again before I pass, my darling little Sophia." As Roger whispers his wishes, Sophia falls into a deep sleep…

CHAPTER ELEVEN

The ship is rocking back and forth as it caresses the roll of the waves. Sophia awakes from her slumber. Yet another day goes by at sea. The distance from her family is straining her good nature. This feels too real now. The separation has turned the spirit of adventure into a battle to stay focused on her journey. Sophia becomes restless. Fear surrounds her with questions that pierce her innocence, like barbed wire. "Where am I going? Who is to care for me? What is to become of me?"

She sits up in her cot and views out of the tiny porthole. The water is lapping at the window. It won't be long now before the ship ports at its destination. Her lip begins to quiver as tears well up and silently roll over her cheeks. Sophia's wisdom grasps hold of her, and lets her know, while this journey is unknown, it *is* her destiny. There is no way around it.

"Come with me," she hears, as she is compelled to go up on deck. The ship is continuing its gentle roll up and down the crest of each wave. Young Sophia walks out to the railing and feels one ray of sunshine break through the clouds. It embraces her and reassures her of the path ahead. In the distance she sees land, from above she feels warmth and guidance. "You are ready, seek Truth, in order to reach your potential," she hears. She smiles at the strength of those words...they warm her heart....she believes the words have magical powers, and those words give her the strength she requires to keep moving forward along this unknown journey.

As the ship nears port, three great white birds come to welcome them in, almost as if they are escorting the ship into dock. They are curious and playful in the way they outfly each other to get a closer look at the ship and its precious cargo.

Sophia runs below deck, quickly gathers her few belongings and heads back up toward the gangway. As she walks down the plank, fear grips her again. The crowd is large and loud at the harbor, but she does not see anyone waiting for her. There are no signs with her name on it. No one is yelling to welcome her. Nothing looks familiar. The smells are even foreign. She has no idea of where to go or what to do now that she's ashore.

Sophia stands alone at the pier for a long time. The crowd slowly dwindles as strangers meet their passengers, and traders exchange their goods. She sits on the wooden dock waiting for someone to come show her the way. Tears begin to mound and spill over her cheeks once again. She's alone, for the first time she allows fear to speak for her as her mumbles grow into quiet anger, "I have no one. I really am left here alone. What was Dad thinking? How could he just let me go so easily? And Astar, huh....she practically ran me onto the ship."

Sophia sinks her head into the palms of her hands and sobs silently. Each salty tear is robbing the sweetness of her intended adventure. She follows her tears as they drop and vanish into the crevices of the crusty old dock.

Then, for a moment, she becomes distracted from her tears. She notices shadows moving upon the old wooden planks. The shadows are of three birds, the same great white birds that were greeting the ship earlier. They are continuing their playful flight right above her. The three are so comical yet persistent in circling around her that it makes her smile again. The birds tumble and soar in their flying games.

She watches them fly up one particular path, on the hill in front of her. They return to her repeatedly; swooping up the right side and turning down the left side of the hill in a glorious figure-8 pattern.

Her inner voice echoes back to her, "These three are your guides, go with them." She hesitantly gathers her few belongings and slowly begins the long walk up the dirt path. The three birds are leading the way, with young Sophia now in tow.

The path quickly clears of merchants, sailors and laborers. Soon Sophia is alone on her way up the mountain. It is just her and her new found friends.

The sun is bright and powerful, as it lingers directly overhead. The uphill climb is slow and the altitude is becoming noticeable in Sophia's breath. She sits back on a large granite stone to rest, but nervously looks for the birds that are directing this part of her travels. She spots two of them perched on the bough of a tree.

While Sophia continues to scan the area for her third guide, she notices a very old woman struggling with a group of young vagrants that seemed to appear out of nowhere. They are surrounding her and overtaking this vulnerable old woman. In their efforts to separate her from her belongings, they are jostling her around very roughly.

Sophia can't stand to see this terrible attack on the elderly woman. Without giving it another thought, she grabs a long stick and enters into the center of the crowd. She begins swinging the stick and yelling, "Get back! Get away, leave her alone!"

The crowd disperses quickly, scattering back to the dark corners from which they had emerged. They were more frightened by Sophia's Light than her might.

Sophia runs over to the woman, helping her up off her knees. "May I help you with your bags?" she asks the sweet-faced elder. She is a dear old lady, with curly, snow-white hair and eyes the color of the deepest blue ocean. Her back is hunched over the heavy bags of supplies. She was attempting to carry this load up the hill to her cottage, when the crowd saw her as easy prey.

As the elder woman gathers herself, she says, "Oh my dear little darling, you've brightened my day by helping me out of this jam." She dusts herself off. "I had just stopped to rest, when that group got a little over zealous. Oh they are just young boys, horsing around, but they darn near trampled me.

"You, my dear, are an amazing young girl; you stepped in, where others have turned away. Words alone will not show my gratitude. You will see." When she smiles there is an air of familiarity about her.

Sophia rests her hand gently on the back of the woman; her soft woolen sweater is comforting to the touch. She gently plucks a stray white feather that is embedded in the fibers of the elder's sweater, before she helps carry the groceries into her cottage.

In hopes of getting an invitation to stay and chat a little more, Sophia charms up a conversation. "It's my pleasure to help you ma'am. Can I do anything else for you? Do you need help putting away your goods?"

"My dear, I am so grateful that you stopped to help me. Like I said, you are very special. As much as I would love to have you stay with me for some time, I know you must return to your path. Go now, seek your potential." The old woman says with a twinkle in her eye, and a warm, crinkled smile that could melt chocolate. "Oh, and watch your path, you never know what steps or stones you might encounter in the middle of your journey," she chuckles.

Sophia has no idea what the kind lady is talking about as she imperceptibly rolls her eyes and responds with, "Yes ma'am thanks for the advice." But she smiles at something familiar in the sweet old woman. "I would love to come visit you again, sometime, if that would be ok?"

"My dear, I am with you always, you may visit as you wish. Now run along before it gets dark. You still have a long way to go before you get back home."

"Oh but ma'am, I'm not going home....and I don't even know your name....and I'm not sure if I'm heading in the right direction...." Sophia is trying to get as much out before she is whisked out the front door, as it moans shut with a puff of dust escaping from the cracks.

Sophia hears the old woman giggle again, bringing about her own laughter. "She must live amongst the stars," escapes Sophia's breath. She begins thinking about the elder and how wonderful to be so free and joyful in one's old age, even though the woman had just escaped the darkness that surrounded her a few moments before.

The breeze has picked up and the sun's rays are tickling the treetops. Sophia thinks aloud, "Back onto the path," as she searches the sky for her three guides. They are nowhere to be found. She begins to wonder what to do. "Should I just go back to the harbor? Maybe this is the wrong way?" Doubt begins to take over but then there is a small interruption, just enough to break away from worrying. She hears chirping. It sounds so sweet. She follows the sounds till she finds herself at the entrance of the woods. Sophia stops, looks back at the path from where she has come, and thinks for a moment about running back to the harbor one more time.

The chirping keeps summoning. Then the songstress shows herself....it is unbelievable. How could this be? Sophia holds her hand out to see if it could be true. The sweet little bird flies directly to her. It is amazing. It is *her* robin, the one with the broken wing that she had mended years ago. She brings the robin in close for a kiss. "This is magical," she whispers to the beautiful bird.

Now the robin begins to flutter around Sophia, filling her with great joy. She chases the robin, following her up the hill. Sophia is laughing and chasing that red robin so far up the hill that she doesn't realize the distance that they have actually climbed. They are deep in the woods and the sun is quietly nestling behind the big trees for the coming night.

Her companion is sitting in the long shadow of a pine, resting from the uphill road they just traversed. The robin senses the concern and worry creeping back into Sophia's mind. She flies over to Sophia's shoulder, nuzzles her cheek and sends this message out to her, "Remain on this path, my darling little Sophia. Fear nothing; the Spirit of Love will give you wings." Those words rekindle memories, for this was the same message Sophia had shared with this little bird so long ago. Just then her feathered messenger flies out of sight as suddenly as she had appeared, leaving Sophia alone again with her thoughts.

It's getting dark, and cold. Sophia tries to start a campfire, but everything is too damp deep within the woods. There is nothing around that resembles kindling for a fire. She gathers up some pine needles and leaves to make a soft spot to settle in for the night. Throwing her pack down, she tries to calm her shaky nerves. The cold and fear are battling for her attention most of the night, until sheer exhaustion wins over both. She falls asleep on the cold, damp leaves. The chatter of her teeth knocking together from the cold was the last thing she heard before finally giving in and falling asleep for the night.

●●●

As dawn slowly awakens the forest, Sophia has the sensation she is surrounded by warmth. "It's so hot," she grumbles. The sleep slowly wears off as she tries to reconcile waking in the cold, morning dew, with feeling so warm, actually hot. Now she's fully awake. She feels the warmth alright! It is warm breath, on her hair!! She jumps to her feet, ready to defend herself when she sees a remarkable sight.

Her warm intruder is a timber wolf that had found her shivering in the darkness. He had surrounded her with his body and breathed warm air for her during the night. She connects eyes with this mighty beast. "This is extraordinary," she thinks. Once again she feels the thread of trust, and she knows it's safe to approach him. He allows her to lay her hand on him, and run it down to his chest. The wolf can sense Sophia's perplexity. "Could it be? Could this be the wolf I saved?" Her fingers feel the scars she had helped heal. The wolf leans in for a familiar nuzzle. Sophia bursts into tears and expresses her joy, "Oh my dear friend, it is so good to see you have fully recovered!" She throws herself around his neck as they nudge each other's foreheads together.

He stands and rubs up against the back of Sophia's legs, coaxing her to follow him. He assures her that he will guide her to her destination. She can barely contain the trust, joy and gratitude to have such a companion alongside on her unknown journey. The hearty wolf stays close to Sophia as they make their way deeper into the woods.

Their journey is an all-day adventure, with stops for berries and sips from the babbling brook that meanders in and out of the path, or what might have been a path if anyone actually came up this way. The wolf knows exactly where to step though; he attentively shows Sophia which stones are safe, and which ones would cause a slip and slide into yesterday. All the while, Sophia keeps hearing the advice of the elder woman in the cottage, to keep mindful for the steps and stones in her path.

It is a long and exhausting hike, all up hill, as they make their way to a beautiful clearing....a meadow, much like the one back home, only much, much bigger. The flowers are even bigger and more colorful. They are dancing to the music of the wind, releasing their sweet essence. The sun glistens off their subtle petals as dew drops quench their thirst. "What a picture this is!" She thinks to herself, remembering her own little meadow back home.

On the far side of the meadow they reach a fork in the road. From a distance, Sophia notices something reflective in the middle of the path. She walks up closer and brushes away the leaves and dirt to fully reveal the mystery. Surprised, yet smiling Sophia is reminded of the elderly woman once again. "A stone, in the middle of my path....with my mystery symbol on it! Pretty amazing, we are in the middle of nowhere. Who could have put this stone here? Was it the old woman? How did she know about the symbols? But she did mention the stone. That old girl couldn't have beaten us all the way up this path, could she?" Sophia quietly questions in amazement as her fingers trace around the precious symbol:

As if to convince herself, she declares aloud, "The stone is a marker! It has to be. It identifies the fork in the road. It's time for a decision." She spans the full view of both trails. One path looks wide open with plenty of food and water, the trail meanders softly, downhill all the way. Maybe it leads back into town where she could get a warm meal, and send a message home. She could go back and forget all about these wild dreams, but she quickly realizes these "wild dreams" are hers to live out. Even though the downhill path would be the easy way out, her companion guides her toward the steep and arduous climb. She trusts the wolf to guide her to her destination. She trusts the wolf with her life.

He gently tugs on her shirt tail toward the path on the right, which continues uphill from here, with the sunlight beaming brightly all the way to the top. Sophia admires the stone once more before placing it into her shirt pocket for safe keeping.

As they fall into a steady pace, Sophia begins to wonder about this stone and the symbols that keep entering her life's path. She looks back onto the events of her life, focusing in on the appearance of these symbols. "Why are these symbols around me? Why have they appeared, but not revealed their meaning? Are these symbols truly indicators?   Are they to guide me? Why am I picked for this quest? And how *did* that little old woman know I would find a stone in my path?" She begins to seek clarity and understanding.

As she finds a rhythmic cadence, a vision begins to unfold before her. She becomes eager to find any clues to her future within the images that begin to weave into day-dreams with each step forward...

The path ahead is bright and sunny.   There is a cold crispness in the air. I hear the crunch of the loose gravel under my steps as I begin up the trail. The sun's rays seem as though they are following me up the path. Each leaf in the trees is casting its very own shadow that glides and dances to the rhythm of my steps. The farther I go into the woods, the more heightened my senses become. The colors of the leaves are flashing before me like fireworks on the 4th of July. The smell of the woods fills my every breath as I exert my way up the climb. I find berries that are bigger and redder than I've ever seen, and they taste oh so sweet!

I then walk over to a big boulder, lean over it and dip my hand into the crystal clear depths of the mountain spring. The water is refreshing and quenches my thirst but soon the cold cramps my fingers. As I pull my hand out of the spring, I see a stone with a carving on it. Then I distinctly hear the word

'Trust'. As soon as I reach into the spring to touch the stone, I hear, 'Gratitude'. The word just enters my mind without any effort. I pull the stone from the water and dry it off. I notice markings on both sides. One side shows my first symbol 𝄢 and on the other side, it displays the second 𝄢. 'Joy', I receive the word as a robin flutters around me. I am filled with joy. I now begin visualizing all the moments of joy, trust, and gratitude that make up my life. The images are hanging in front of me like a string of pearls: my mother's voice, I hear it, while in the womb. Mom sings to me, 'You are my sunshine....' all the time while rubbing her belly during pregnancy. Then I see visions of the golden sun shedding its light and showing the wisdom of Nature to me every day that I am able to explore my surroundings back home. Oh, and the warmth I feel in the protective arms of my father. And Astar too! Where to begin? I think Astar may have known me even before I was born."

The vision fades as Sophia brings Astar to her forethought; a wispy dream-like image of Astar speaks, "Remember when I would tell you the story of how Love brought me to the hospital the day you were born? I was there for a reason...to guide you. Like the North Star guides the three Magi...the wisest ones upon the land". Astar's distant voice directs Sophia then fades into the wind.

Meanwhile Sophia and the wolf have come upon a scene to behold. Her little friend, the red robin materializes, as if from thin air, and lands on her shoulder with a gentle flap of her wings. Her dear wolf friend is once again supporting her and nudging behind her calves to keep Sophia moving forward.

Sophia looks up ahead. "It's the scene from Astar's fairytales!" she exclaims in awe. "Astar would describe this place to me, in detail, in almost every story." There is something mystical about the view. Beyond where she's standing, is a huge meadow. This one filled with multi-colored flowers that turn their faces toward the light of the sun. It is a spectacular garden of light, as the sun's rays penetrate between the majestic trees to bounce off the petals of every bloom. In the distance, at the far end of the meadow, stands a cute little cottage, much like the one owned by the little old woman that Sophia helped the day before, except, this house looks as if it is made entirely from pink stone. Behind the house is a hill and atop the hill is a sole tree--big, sturdy and beautiful. Its branches are embracing the message the wind is carrying. Through the stillness, Sophia can make out the whispers, "Seek Truth."

Sophia is emboldened by the whispering wind. She begins her courageous walk through the meadow, listening to the singing of the birds and crickets alternating as she approaches the garden gate surrounding the cottage. From this viewpoint, the stones of the cottage appear to be pink alabaster. There is a craggily old tree just inside the gate. Its crusty distortion adds to its beauty. One of its branches distinctly points toward the front door of the cottage. This limb is bent and weathered; it looks like the crooked finger of a wise old sage pointing the way to one's future.

Sophia realizes how slow she has been moving through the meadow when she notices that dusk has tiptoed in behind her. With the darkness lurking, she is unsure of her next steps, yet she knows neither Astar nor the wolf would misguide her.

She feels fully present in this time and space. "This must be the right way," she encourages herself.

Once again Sophia musters her courage then opens the gate with a creak so loud it quiets all the crickets at once. The silence becomes frightening as she takes a step forward. The spring-loaded gate slams shut behind her with such a crack that it scares off her two guides and best companions, deep into the woods.

She has to take these next steps alone. Her knees are knocking together in fear, as she takes another step toward the front door. The stepping stone she is standing on wobbles as if to focus Sophia's attention back onto her path. She looks down and notices it is not a stone at all. It is a big, thick, round, iron disk, with rust and dirt embedded deep into its crevices. Her surroundings are definitely getting darker now; she can barely make out the symbol on the iron disk. She kicks at some of the loose dirt. Her eyes dart around a jagged image. "The 5-pointed star—a pentagram!"

Fear grabs at her feet and turns her around. This symbol invokes great fear in those who see it. Her imagination is in control now. She thinks all five points of the star are stabbing her feet as she turns to pull feverishly at the gate. As much as she tries, it won't open. She becomes frantic and looks up to the heavens to seek help. Just as Sophia scans the deep blue sky, looking for guidance, the answer glistens into view. There it is, up in the twilight sky, big, bright, and as powerful as ever—her North Star. Sophia clearly hears Astar's voice upon the wind with a stern, "Get your wits about you girl! Don't run away now. It is time for you to grow up young lady. Go forward. You are ready. This is your dream, your will, your *right*!"

Sophia calms down, and slowly composes herself. As she turns to face the cottage, she notices an oil lamp is now burning through the window of the cottage, making the entire home glow with a warm pearly hue. This comforts her, a lot.

She wipes her nose and dries her eyes. "Courage," she tells herself while tracing her footsteps back to the iron disk. Now the symbol is clearly seen in the light cast by the rising full moon. What she mistakenly thought was a pentagram, is really a *six*-pointed star. Actually, it is two inter-locking triangles, a darker one pointing south to the gate and the path from where she had just arrived. Then a lighter triangle is pointing north to the front door of the cottage, toward where she is heading.

Looking around on the ground, she notices a few of these stepping stones. Each one has a different symbol on it. On her initial pass toward the front door, she had stepped over the first stone entirely, but now she can see every step, from the gate to the entry door. Upon each stone there is a distinct symbol. She goes back to the beginning and views each symbol in order:

 An old Egyptian-looking symbol is on the first stone disk, closest to the gate.

The double triangles, that are interlocked, are next on the rusty iron disk.

Further on there is a directional, whirling cross that reminds Sophia of the four winds of Nature. It is on a copper disk that has a beautiful patina of blues and greens.

Last is a dark, mystic circle whose circumference is barely visible with the naked eye. It appears on a disk made of unrecognizable stone.

Sophia then approaches the front door of the cottage and the final symbol comes into view:

The symbol is hanging on the heavy wooden door. It is a glorious ornament, mostly made of black glass and partly made of what looks like…gold. As she nears the door she is fully aware this ornament is the same beautiful symbol she had been guided to create back at home. She follows the large ebony "S" with her eyes, until a sudden stop at the golden "i"…the dot on top of the letter is missing. When she gingerly touches the vacant spot, she feels a warm sensation atop her heart. She looks down to see a muffled glow from her shirt pocket. Upon reaching in she discovers the stone she had found along her path is a golden glow and warm to the touch.

"Incredible," she whispers to herself as she takes the stone from her pocket and notices that it is changing. She turns the stone and examines both sides, only to find that the symbol is now connected, it forms the figure-8. She instinctively moves the stone toward what appears to be its rightful resting place. Sophia then gently places it in the missing dot of the 'i'. The moment the stone connects the golden "i" with the ebony "S", the entire symbol turns a crystalline blue and the door magically swings open. The inviting light of the lamp guides Sophia in from the dark. Once inside the cottage, she hears someone's voice from the hearth, "Come in my dear, we've been expecting you."

Sophia moves in closer to the center of the room, looking around curiously. The cottage is small and cozy, with a welcoming feeling. There's a tinkering at the fireplace where Sophia sees her host for the first time, but only from behind. "Sit down my dear. We thought you would *never* get in here." A sweet old voice giggles as she turns to serve up two cups of tea.

"It's *you!*" Sophia rushes to help the cute old woman with the tea cups. "How did you get here? That mountain trail is so steep and long, how could you have gotten here? Who are you? What is your name? You are so sweet and kind, and your face...it's so much like...oh, I don't know, but I must know! You look so familiar to me, not just from our meeting yesterday, but I've been thinking about you a lot, and you look like I should know you, and..." Sophia would continue with a thousand more questions if she wasn't interrupted.

"Oh my darling little Sophia, I look familiar to you because we are all connected my dear. We are children of the stars, each one of us, and we all have that star fire within us. That is what you see so clearly in me, because it is so powerful within you too."

Sophia is surprised that her host knows her name, "Ma'am, I'm sure we didn't get a chance to introduce ourselves. So, um, how do you know my name?"

"Come and sit down with me, drink some tea to settle yourself, and we can begin to unravel this mystery together."

Sophia is completely drawn to this woman. Her smile is an open invitation for understanding, and Sophia can't wait to hear everything that is about to be shared.

"My name is Rose. I am an Elder, one of many that you will encounter throughout your life. I will be here to inspire you to connect with all the treasures deep within you." As Rose finishes these words, a robin flies in the window and sits upon Rose's shoulder. "Remember your little friend?" Rose asks Sophia as she scoops up the bird and places her onto Sophia's extended hand. "My dear, this was the first time you recognized your own power, wasn't it? You healed this little songstress with your love. That's when we knew for sure that you have been nurturing your innate powers."

Sophia cups the robin in her hands and brings her close to her cheek as joy fills her heart. "My 'innate powers', what powers could *I* have? I'm simply a girl. I did what anyone would have done to help a creature in need." Just as she diminishes her skills, new images of her mother begin coming to life, appearing as holograms upon white light, one after the other. "Are you doing this?" After a slight pause, "Am *I* doing this?" She asks in wonder, smiling as the images pick up speed and begin to move like an old-time movie.

Then the image of her mother begins to speak, "Sophia, sweetheart, you are so kind and gentle and beautiful. Your expressive soul is even lovelier than I had envisioned. I want you to know that I am with you always along this sacred path. I too will help guide you. You are not alone. You will know I am near by the sway of the wind, kissing your forehead and singing you songs. I have been watching in wonder as your beauty manifests in your actions. We are so proud of you, and we know you will do what is true for you. Continue to seek

Truth. It is your destiny." Her voice fades on the evening breeze, summoning the images after it.

Rose can sense the love in Sophia's eyes, as she offers a glimmer of Hope, "Your mother is an angel."

"Yes, Rose. My dad often tells me that about her." Sophia softly confesses, longing to have known her mother as others had.

Rose takes Sophia's hands into her own wrinkled palms and once again states, "Listen to what I am saying my dear. Your mother *is an angel*. Once we shared the entire vision with her, she knew that she would have more freedom to express her love for you and your father as an angel. Possessing this knowledge made her choice, to have you come through their lives, while giving up her own, more acceptable to her reasoning mind."

Sophia begins sobbing. For the first time, she comprehends her mother's sacrifice, as she deeply mourns her loss. A warm breeze swirls around Sophia, before she begins to celebrate the confirmation that the angelic visions of her mother are real. During Sophia's entire life, her mother has appeared to her as this exquisitely beautiful angel.

Just as Sophia is about to breakdown within this turmoil of emotions once again, she gets bumped up behind her legs, hard enough to jolt her back into the present moment. It's her best companion, the timber wolf.

As Sophia bends over to nuzzle her head onto the chest of the wolf, Rose continues, "Sophia, the Elders have been with you since before your birth. The promise had been delivered, that a star child would come to us soon. The Elders informed your parents of their role if they chose to fulfill their calling. The message was so pure that they did not, and could not resist having you come into their lives. They courageously agreed, even though each one, individually through differing visions of their own, had seen the outcome of their choice long before committing to it.

The Elders know you possess the grace and strength to be given the keys to the Truth. Early on, we were enlightened to your potential. Therefore, we sent watchers, guides and messengers along your path."

When Rose mentions the 'watchers' the wolf pokes his head under Sophia's hand, as if asking her to understand that he has been with her always, watching out for her. The robin, wanting to be recognized as her 'messenger', begins to sing as Rose interrupts with, "Yes, my sweet songstress, we'll tell her about Astar, too."

"Tell me what about Astar?" Sophia is curious as to how Rose knows about Astar at all. No mention of her dear friend and caregiver has been made before now.

"Astar is one of us, my dear, an Elder, a guide, *your* guide. When we knew you were seeded by the stars, we needed you to have a guiding light to nurture and protect you on your path. We also had to give your dear father a soft place to fall for his brave commitment to this journey, Sophia. Now, it is time to take you into *our* fold, to inform you of the depth and breadth of this great Wisdom that resides within, this Spirit of Love.

"Make no mistake though, this decision is yours to make. You can choose if you want to enter within us, or turn back. There is no wrong decision my sweet darling. Your intuition will guide you now. Trust your inner voice. I will leave you to your thoughts. Drink your tea and tell me your decision as it reveals itself to you. Goodnight dearie."

Rose putters toward a raised area in the cottage, she pulls back a veil of midnight-blue fabric and ducks back behind it, warmly expressing again, "Goodnight dearie, sweet dreams."

Sophia takes a sip of the tea, while she takes in everything she's just seen and heard. As she brings the teacup to her lips for another sip, she slowly slips into her own dreamy cloud where an apparition of Astar appears, sipping from her butterfly-handle tea cup.

The image comfortably nestles into her favorite over-stuffed chair in the den at Hope's Haven. It looks as if Astar is viewing out of the window onto the changing colors of the autumn foliage back home. She begins speaking to Sophia in her dream-bound state, "Sophia my girl, I'm here to let you know that once you express your will, the Universe will conspire with each and every atom to help you reach your destiny. I believe in you sweet child. Follow your heart."

CHAPTER TWELVE

The morning sun beams into the cottage very early. The rays ignite a dance amongst the particles floating in the light. Sophia awakens to the gentle movement of the dust particles, and is mesmerized by the beauty of their swirling energy. She sits up in the chair that cradled her night's sleep, and feels the warmth of her wolf friend lying across her feet.

The robin jumps onto her shoulder then both the robin and the wolf begin to express their joy. They sense something, even before Sophia is awake enough to know it within herself. Sophia laughs aloud at the sight. The strong wolf looks simply giddy as he is chasing his tail in one direction then turning to chase it in another merry circle, while the robin is fluttering from side to side as if she is on an imaginary swing.

The midnight-blue veil that Rose disappeared behind last night has enchantingly turned into the shade of clear morning skies. There is some rustling behind the veil before Rose appears again. "May the sun shine its love and light to each of you this splendid morning." She greets them with a basket of warm home-baked goodies that smell as if angels created the sweet morsels. "Sophia, since you're staying with us, you may as well put the kettle on the fire. We need to celebrate your wise decision."

"Rose, I must stay. I can't even imagine turning back now, but how did you all know that my decision has been made?" Sophia asks with probing interest as she swings the kettle full of water toward the hearth of the fireplace. Just as she swings the kettle into position, the fire leaps up with arms of flames that hug the kettle, widening Sophia's eyes in amazement.

Rose giggles again, "My dear, there is so much to learn, the kettle fire is child's play. In time, you will understand more about your gifts, and what you will want for yourself and all those you touch. Oh, you asked how we knew your decision was made. That secret is written across your heart, and your smile reveals it to all."

Sophia is enchanted by this dear woman. Rose possesses the same kindness that Astar shares with everyone she meets. They are both vessels of love.

CHAPTER THIRTEEN

The moon is huge and full, hanging low in the night sky. Roger secretly mixes himself another heavy-handed cocktail, before walking out to the kitchen porch. He peers from above onto Hope's rose garden. It used to be filled with fragrant flowers, but he has let the weeds in. They are beginning to take hold. They are beginning to choke out the beauty that used to grow freely here.

During his nightly attempts to drown out his loneliness, he bitterly tosses out the half-melted ice from his cocktail glass onto the thirsting flowerbeds. He has turned his back on their growth, and his.

Astar is up in the attic, rummaging around for something in particular. "I know I've seen you around here, now show yourself." she mumbles aloud. "Ah-ha, there you are." She grabs an old tattered roll of papers. "This should do the trick."

As she stands up with the roll, she notices the moon through the attic window. The silvery disk appears larger than usual and is hanging low in the evening skyline. It has a bright ring of light around it as a zephyr dances with clouds in front of the reflecting orb. Astar smiles knowingly, "I knew you could do it sweetheart."

She puts the roll of papers over her shoulder and makes her way down the stairs. "Roger, come quickly," she commands. When Roger arrives, she slams the roll of papers onto the kitchen table and exclaims, "Our little girl has accepted her challenge, and now you must accept yours."

Roger's eyes fill with tears that threaten to dissolve his hardened heart, as the news of Sophia settles in. "She's doing it? She's staying there? How long will she be gone?"

Astar gives Roger a reassuring hug, "She's in good hands Roger. No need to worry. Just keep busy and this time will fly by; I promise this to you." She begins to unravel the roll. The papers are blueprints. They are the plans for the mansion Roger was going to build with Hope. "I've been thinking that you will need a hobby in the meantime. You know what they say about idle hands? So, here you go. Have at it! It's time to put down the bottle and pick up a hammer, son."

Astar is downright demanding in her encouragement, to have Roger begin construction of this home. She can immediately see the result of pulling Roger away from his provocative mistress of intoxication, as he inches closer to the blueprints with interest.

One thing Astar knows for sure is that this home is meant to be built, right here, on this forty-acre parcel called Hope's Haven.

Roger scoffs at the idea though. No way is he about to embark on this project; it will take years to bring it to life. But soon his sneer turns into a smirk, and then a smile, as he exchanges his drinking glass for his reading glasses. He opens the plans and begins turning the pages, viewing in deep detail the next several years of his life. "Thank you for letting me know of Sophia's choice. I guess we always knew our little girl would do it. She is so damn curious about all that life has to offer. She wouldn't know how to turn away from them--the Elders, and their mystical stories. And Astar...well...I just want to say, thank you...for saving me....again."

CHAPTER FOURTEEN

The warmth of the morning sun is awakening the forest. The energy is gathering momentum as the news of Sophia's decision swells throughout the woodlands. The faithful robin sends the message to the flowers, who whisper it to the bees and soon their sweet nectar quietly informs the bears and so the news goes forth throughout the depths of the woods. The chatter amongst the creatures in the wilderness is spreading beyond the Garden of Light, just as two loud thuds are heard on the roof above the cottage window, followed by a few bird squawks.

Rose chuckles perceptively, "Now that we are all here, I will begin. Sophia, my dear, you have spent the first twelve years guided by the light of Astar, our Elder sister from the North. This next period you will grow with us, the Elders of the East, South and West."

Sophia looks around curiously wondering who Rose is referring to, as no other 'Elder' is in the room. Just then two bright white feathers float into the cottage, landing at Sophia's feet as she places the morning tea on the table.

Sophia crouches down, picks up the feathers and holds them up to the ray of light coming through the open window. As she does, she sees two of her three white-feathered guides from the docks. The birds are gorgeous up close. They enter into the cottage as though they have done this often, and comfortably seat themselves around the breakfast table.

Rose continues, "We three are here to convey the truth for you to judge as you see fit. We are here to simply lift the veil; the rest is up to you my dear. While we are referred to as the Elders, we too are students of our ancient history. We faithfully choose to accept the teaching as it comes across our path, just as you are choosing to do so."

Sophia is eager to learn. In her true form, she is bursting with questions. "What am I to learn? What am I to do with all this wisdom? Why me? Why have I been chosen? "

Just as she stops to fill her lungs for the next barrage of inquiries, Rose interjects. "Oh sweet child, over time, you will uncover the answers to all your questions, and discover many new ones to take their place. It delights the Universe to see a curious soul. Ask your questions about life, all of it. Never shy away from seeking Truth." Rose cradles Sophia's smiling face in her caring hands. "There may be moments when these next seven years will feel like seven times seven, and then there may come moments when the answers will flow through you like water quenching your thirst. Be patient with yourself and with us, listen to your intuition, then this Wisdom will shine from within you."

"I have so many more questions, Rose, but first I need to know: What about my father? When can I see him? I promised that I would return to him. Can he come visit me?" Sophia has not quite absorbed the level of her commitment; it is slowly sinking in that this part of her path will take *several years*. As the understanding fills her senses, she whispers, "I guess I will see him in due time. Will I be able to send him messages, at least?"

"Sophia darling, send your messages on the winds of the Universe. Once your father finds his mode of connection, he will receive each one of them, clearly."

The great white birds begin cooing as Rose continues, "He is in great hands my dear child. Astar has put him to work, and you will be so proud of his creation. But he will need time to perfect his craft, as will you. Just as your intuition informs you, you will see him in due time. Know that your love binds the two of you together, and nothing will ever diminish that sacred love.

"Ah, sacred love...what a wonderful way to begin. Let's drink our tea and enter into life's wonderful mystery." The great white birds eagerly flap their wings as they witness the art of discovery about to unfold.

While watching their movement, Sophia notices a small alcove, with an oil lamp that has been burning throughout the night. In an effort to be helpful, she walks over to the bright light, and asks, "Should I put out the fire in this lamp?" She attempts to blow out the flame. The flame dances, but doesn't blow out. Sophia tries to extinguish it again, but the radiance of the flame cannot be diminished.

Rose gives her crinkled smile while watching Sophia trying to do the impossible. She walks over to the alcove and puts her arm around Sophia's shoulders, "My dear the fire shall never go out. It burns forever..."

"...a fire that burns forever!? How can this be, Rose? Is it a trick? How can a flame burn forever? How does it work, really? Is the flame for this poem in the alcove? Did you write this, Rose?" Then Sophia slowly reads the writing on the parchment, aloud:

The Infinite

Reflects

Creation

With the Divine forces of Mother Nature

To evolve spirit and matter

Through all forms of life

In order to reveal the sacred Truth

Silence fills the room as Sophia feels the electric impulse of the words in every atom of her being. The energy surrounding her feels like she's bathing under a waterfall of effervescence. "Rose this poem is beautiful, but I don't really understand it, not completely. It's strange, I connect with it so strongly, but I don't know why." Sophia tries to explain what she means, "You know that feeling on Christmas morning, when you get your first bicycle? You're filled with joy and excitement at getting everything you could have ever wanted, even though you are aware that you don't even know how to ride it!"

Rose laughs out loud, "Yes, my dear, that's to be expected. But you will soon be racing around the world on this bicycle."

Sophia's inquisitive mind begins again, "Clearly this poem is dear to you. You've placed it in this special nook in the heart of your home, with a fire that burns forever! *Forever*? What do you mean a fire that burns forever? Can you tell me more, can you tell me *anything*?"

Rose is amused by Sophia's energy and curiosity as she explains, "About the writing, I can tell you this: These are not my words, but the words of ancient Wisdom, handed down through time. It is for you to seek the truth behind the words. Once you have discovered it, the secret of the eternal fire will be held within you too. Know that it is your personal journey to connect with the Spirit of this poem.

"My dear, the Wisdom will come to you over time. I know this to be true. It is close within reach for all who seek it. We are merely guides. One day, you will gain the knowledge behind these words. It is then that your journey home will begin, in order to experience this great Wisdom."

Rose enters into the next seven years, from the very beginning. She starts with the very first step as one enters the Garden of Light. She raises her right hand and draws up some of the glowing dust particles that have been dancing in the morning sunlight. She casts the glittering dust onto the table in front of Sophia.

The golden shimmer perfectly forms the symbol of Life:

The trick frightens and excites Sophia at the same time. "How did you do that?" Sophia is inspired to listening intently. Slowly she realizes that the answers to her questions will come in time.

Rose begins, "Let's start with the first symbol inside the Garden of Light. The 'T' is an ancient symbol representing the Tree of Life. Life is where we gain the knowledge of good and evil--love and fear.

"This is the first stone you crossed over when you came into the Garden of Light. You stepped right over it during your courageous quest for Truth, maybe because this first step has come so easily for you. Does this symbol look familiar to you?"

"Yes Rose, it sure does, from the stones in your garden. The first stone has this 'T' with a circle above it. Tell me more." Sophia is fully engaged as she feels the electric impulse surround her as though it is a hug from the heavens.

"Our friends are near." Whispers Rose as she too feels the heavenly charged hug! "The Tree of Life is our body, mind and soul. The discernment of love and fear is our journey, and the connection with the Infinite Spirit of Love is our potential. We are churning knowledge into experience, and experience into wisdom. It's a mystical cycle of learning my dear."

"So then, this 'T' represents life, each one of us, making our way through the Universe? We each have free will to choose our own path, but the way home is clearest when we choose love over fear?" Sophia wants to gain assurance she's on the right path. "Then, what does the circle tell us? What does it mean?"

An unfamiliar, yet soft spoken voice chimes in, "The circle represents the spirit. The 'T' represents the material life. This beautiful symbol, when united, represents our true potential: The triumph of Love over fear." The voice comes from a gorgeous, dark-complexioned woman, with high cheek bones and warm almond-shaped eyes. She is inexplicably sitting in the place of one of the great white birds.

Sophia is sitting, wide-eyed with astonishment. She gazes in wonder at the beauty that now sits across from her. While her mind attempts to understand the transformation of a bird into this woman, right before her eyes, she observes another Elder reveal himself in the same mystic way.

He begins by passing this Wisdom to Sophia, "This spirit is dwelling within you my dear. All created form has the spirit within. Over time and space we gain knowledge and experience. Through our thoughts, our words, and our actions we resonate with all that surrounds us, in ways we can't yet imagine! The will of each individual, every family and all nations affects the spirit of the Universe. You see our thoughts, words and actions manifest, attract and coalesce; then, they crystallize to create this world in which we all live. When fear consumes our intent, the world becomes heavy with control and greed. Fear hardens our hearts for our brothers and sisters and makes us react in ways we would not tolerate in others, yet fear is allowed to run wild in ourselves."

He stands and walks over to the poem in the alcove. He adjusts the lamp of forever flame and then continues, "When we connect with the Spirit of Love, the souls of each of us and the soul of the Universe become enlightened." His words are as powerful as his stature.

Miraculously, the two birds had transformed themselves to become her Elder guides. The love that surrounds Sophia banishes any fear of the unknown.

Rose reaches over and places one hand on Sophia's and the other on the hand of the stunning, young woman sitting across from her, "Sophia, this beautiful soul is named Ama.

She is an Elder from the West, and she is here to guide you."
Then Rose reaches for the tall, chiseled-chin man who has
made his way back to his seat at the table. "This excessively
handsome man is Naseem, an Elder from the East, who will
also guide your journey. Now that we have begun, let's
continue to reveal the potential of seeking Truth."

Sophia is bewildered and speechless as she visually
explores the new guests. Ama is a tall, young woman with
magnificent flowing hair, graceful eyes and a subtle touch.
When she speaks, it is as if warm waters cleanse over your
awaiting thoughts and leave you in a state of purity and bliss.

Naseem is handsome beyond words. His rugged yet
supportive verses wrap around you like the autumn winds, and
guide you toward your highest potential.

These next seven years will be written in the pages of time
as Sophia adeptly becomes an active seeker of Truth. She is
eager to string together all the pearls of Wisdom the Elders
dare to reveal.

CHAPTER FIFTEEN

Roger has resumed his nightly walks to Hope's mighty oak. He walks beneath the canopy of leaves and leans his back against its robust trunk. Gently his head falls back towards the tree till it comes to rests atop the symbol Sophia had created: ∞

A warm sensation emanates throughout Roger's body. He jumps away from the tree and turns toward it. Again, a ray of light is teasingly calling him forth. Roger approaches with cautious inquiry. Once his fingers connect with the glow of light from the symbol, messages and stories of love begin to recite in Sophia's voice. The experience expands into visions. The images are vivid, colorful, and real, just as if Roger is experiencing each tale through Sophia's own eyes.

Roger has found the portal to Sophia. This beautiful symbol that Sophia used to connect herself to her parents is now the mode of connection and communication between them. He can hear her rapid fire exhilaration in all her messages. The winds of the Universe have kept their promise to deliver the thoughts she sends to her father. He can even smell the angelic scent of the home-baked goodies as Sophia retells the events of the day she made her decision to stay with the Elders. He feels the warmth of her tears on his own cheeks as she tells of how the wolf has been her 'watcher' all along. He senses their bond of trust, he feels his own personal connection with this wolf too, for 'we are *all* connected', is the message that vibrates around him.

Roger is completely lucid when his connection with the wolf reveals itself so vividly in his mind's eye. The gunshot the wolf received through the heart was as material as the one Roger received when the news of Hope's passing exploded into his reality, years ago. He and the wolf share one common link--Sophia. It has taken her love and caring to mend both their shattered hearts. Their bond of trust with Sophia, had been established the moment their eyes met with hers.

These three hearts will always be connected to each other. Roger, Sophia and the timber wolf are a trinity of courage.

Gratitude fills his heart as the messages from Sophia fill his mind. The Love enlightens and vitalizes his actions. It gives him the strength he needs to follow through with Astar's insistence on building the mansion at Hope's Haven.

Roger gains strength and focus. He walks around the hilltop with a renewed purpose, peering out to choose picture-perfect viewpoints and faultless rock formations as he gathers the lay of the land. He spends the rest of the day, and deep into the night, surveying the grounds until he identifies the perfect site to plot the home.

The cosmos assure him that his choice is flawless. Just as a gentle breeze kisses the back of his neck, Hope assures him too, "This meadow is where our home will be built."

Roger senses Hope by his side as he proclaims, "We will build this home together, and it will become a beautiful sanctuary for peace."

CHAPTER SIXTEEN

Over the past seven years, every morning before dawn, Sophia leaves the cottage to enter the Garden of Light. She finds a spot under the wise old tree by the gate and sends out her stories and messages of love on the winds of the Universe. The openness of her heart, allows her to correspond freely. With each message sent to her father, his love returns to her like ripples on a still lake.

Once dawn breaks through the treetops she makes her way back into the cottage to be one with the Elders as they continue to convey the wisdom of life to her.

Every day she crosses over each stepping stone from the garden gate to the cottage door. One at a time she ponders the symbols and their individual purpose. Her mind innocently suggests, "They pave the way from the Garden of Light into the heart of the home." Then her heart echoes back, "They guide the soul back to the Garden of Light." She hears the words, but her intuition tells her to reach deeper. "Seek Truth" keeps coming from her inner voice.

This particular morning Sophia makes her way to the wise old tree by the garden gate, and sits quietly beneath it. The soft angelic breeze that brushes her hair and places a kiss upon her forehead each morning arrives; then it too settles itself around Sophia. Her mind is empty of stories, messages or even thoughts. For the first time, her will is calm and hushed. On this day, she just sits, patiently. Nothing is stirring. She watches the fabric of her shirt pulse with each heartbeat. The stillness becomes calmness then it turns to contentment.

From under the tree she patiently watches as the rays of light fall from the sun and find their rightful place upon each of the symbols. The light slowly fractures into every facet of the symbolic steps with the precision of a master gem-cutter. When the sun breaks dawn and momentarily rests upon the back of the highest mountain range, the light beams reveal their gems in unison.

"This is magnificent!" Sophia says aloud. As she leans forward from under the tree and begins to absorb the magic of the moment, she realizes the brilliance she is seeing. "I alone have this view. Today, this very morning, from under this wise old tree, this splendid gift is for me to unwrap." Gratitude begins to surge within Sophia. She feels an all-embracing, all-loving, transfer of energy and knowledge. For the first time, Sophia cannot completely or correctly verbalize this experience, as the words do not exist to express the purity of Love, Truth and Oneness that is being awakened within her.

It is at this precise moment that the light of the sun reflects each individual symbol from the stepping stones, onto the door of the cottage. The reflections sparkle as Wisdom reveals itself! On this day, in the light of the rising sun, the years of gathering knowledge and experience meld into a single moment of clarity for Sophia. An electric charge shoots into her being as she is drawn to the Truth reflected by the Light. The sun makes sense of each individual symbol; each one a gem of Truth, reflecting to Sophia all she has been seeking.

For the first time, Sophia understands the purity of the poem in the alcove. Each symbol, from the first stepping stone to the last one, all of them join together to reveal the meaning and unity of the symbols, the poem, and Infinite Wisdom. This Wisdom reveals the potential of life to Sophia.

An aura surrounds her as she understands the words she had first seen seven years ago. This time, she allows her intuition to place the Wisdom of the words into her awaiting thoughts. As the experience forges into Truth, Sophia declares, "Your Reflection is within me always, and I am a part of You...when united, we are One!"

She is filled with Love as she stands and twirls with all the woodland creatures that gather around the wonderful Light. She continues to dance then she begins to run with pure exhilaration. She is leaping through the Garden of Light. Out the gate she runs, her stride lengthens and picks up speed throughout the meadow. The flowers turn their beautiful blooms toward Sophia's Light as she leaps and dances with joy over her connection with this Truth.

Sophia runs in delight for some time, rejoicing and embracing this splendid experience. It isn't until she finally slows down, that she notices she has twirled her way back into the depths of the forest, only this time she does not have her trusted guide and companion at her side. She has not entered the woods for seven years and the overgrowth is quite noticeable. The sunlight has difficulty making its way through the weighted limbs of the trees, but darkness sneaks in, bringing unfamiliar yet persistent images with it.

Sophia hears voices in need, want, desire and passion, calling out all at once. There is a cold, damp air surrounding her that chills her to the bone. She begins to see visions she has never perceived before. Images of people entrenched with lust, greed, and pride, all bound down by fear. The harsh visions flood her mind: crimes separating our lives into divided kingdoms, races, genders, religions. She sees wars upon freedom of every form taking place, devouring the soul of man and Earth at the same time. The visions capture Sophia's Light and pull it down into the pit of material reality. She can feel the weight of fear entrapping souls and leaving them burdened and motionless in their personal search for Truth.

This frightens her so! She runs back to the edge of the forest where the light of the sun can once again be felt. As she stands in the expanse between the Garden of Light and the pit of darkness, she hears the voices from the depths, once again. They are pained and hoarse with want. The words have no clarity but the longing and suffering is heard in the echoes. The sounds gnash at Sophia's heart. She feels their pain and passion, yet she runs away from their calling voices; engulfed by her own personal fear of what she is experiencing.

"What is happening? How could the light of my connection dim so quickly? I have never felt this type of revulsion and anguish. I must get back to the Garden of Light. I must get back to the Elders, and the Wisdom. Their light will protect me from these horrors." Sophia runs back across the meadow, looking over her shoulder into the darkness for the first time in her life.

"She is not ready!" Naseem states as he turns to Rose and Ama. "We've unveiled all that we can to her, but she turns her back on her potential. She is running away from the Wisdom!"

Astar sends her message to the others from afar, as her deep, concerned voice arrives upon the mystic winds, "Give her time. She is close, I know it."

Rose confirms, "Astar is right, she is close to attainment. Don't forget that Sophia has been sheltered from the weight of the outside world during her youth--growing up in Hope's Haven. Then, she has spent the past seven years here with us, in the Garden of Light. Her fear is to be expected. We need to be patient with her. She is in possession of the knowledge that we have imparted to her, and now she has seen the Light. The Truth has awakened within her. It is up to her to weave this Truth into her future, and bring Light to the darkest of her visions. I believe in her. Hush now, here she comes, let's hear her out."

"Rose, Naseem, Ama, I'm so glad to see you're all together," Sophia blurts out in one rapid-fire exhalation, then stops and leans over the back of the chair to catch her breath.

"Sophia, you're shaking. What has happened? Tell us what you've done!" Naseem asks on the verge of impatience.

Rose walks over and lays a comforting hand upon Sophia, and encourages her to embrace the experience she has just battled through. Then she directs a gentle look of concern toward Naseem, to help him guide his desire for results in a calmer manner.

Sophia begins in the depths of the forest, telling the Elders of the fear she encountered there. She is still bound by her personal fears as she retells her experience in the darkness of the woods. The Love that awakened from within her heart is being overshadowed by this fear even as she speaks in the presence of the Elders.

Ama hugs Sophia and immerses the persistent fears into an ocean of Love as she begins, "Sophia dear, go back. Start with the dawn of this splendid day. You awakened to something deep within you. Connect with that Truth, for it is real. Tell us everything my dear, even the smallest of details. Feel the waters of Love wash away your fears and keep them at bay."

As peace begins to return to Sophia's heart, Naseem surrounds her with a warm breeze of support. They all gently reassure her back to the moment of her great connection, as Naseem begins anew, "You received the seed of Truth today my dear, and it blossomed into a precious flower because you are a vessel of Love. Can you go back to that moment?"

The warmth of Naseem's voice comforts Sophia. She can now invoke this powerful Love he is speaking of, because she recognizes how to connect with it. "Yes!" She responds with the brilliance of the Light she is witnessing once again. "I received the brightest message. One that brings us all together, all of humankind along with Nature herself! On wings of Light, this Wisdom made its connection with my heart."

As Sophia expresses her thoughts, a beautiful violet-chested hummingbird appears. This tiny drop of sweetness is fluttering right over Sophia's head. The flapping of its wings turns the sun-kissed particles of dust into a golden symbol of infinity. The mystical symbol is hovering over Sophia just as the symbol had done back home in her dreams, so many years ago. The Elders smile as this sign confirms that Sophia has fully awakened the Truth within, and recognizes how to connect with it.

Sophia continues, once again filled with Love, "I understand that we truly are never alone. We are all connected, not only to each other, but to every single plant and animal that has ever lived."

As Sophia's aura brightens to crystalline white; her ego attempts to challenge her again. Fear enters her voice, "But I have seen visions that frighten me. What are these images? Why do they dare me to enter the wilderness *alone*? How could I have turned my back on them? Why does this fear darken my light?"

Ama softly offers, "Fear is the mind's response to the thought of failure. Fear does not emanate from the Soul. Know what I say to be pure, and your Light will never be diminished again."

"Ama, I don't know that I can withstand the fear I feel when I am in the wilderness alone. It was different when I was young and my trusted timber wolf was by my side to guide me. Can he be with me again?" Sophia is stumbling while attempting to stay connected with the Truth. This discovery is still so new and the strength of her connection is quite fragile.

Rose interjects, "Sophia, this fear comes from your ego, wanting to regain control of your will from your awakened spirit. Fear comes in a foolish attempt to diminish the purity of Love that you possess within. It comes in order to control your actions and thus alter your destiny. With your personal willpower, ascend and connect to the Spirit, the Divine Will of the Universe." Rose faithfully encourages Sophia.

The guidance dawns upon Sophia, "It is just as the infinity symbol shows me--to stay connected. The symbol is just a reminder. It has always been near me, reminding me to 'Stay connected to the Spirit' and impressing that we are one, united...We are one with this Divine Spirit." She understands the symbol guides her toward her potential by reminding her to stay connected to the awakened Light within—the Spirit of Love. In doing so, she will find the path to healing the anguished voices that call to her from the pit of darkness.

"Rose, Ama, Naseem and Astar--I know you can hear me, too. I believe you have been my sages of Wisdom, protectors of Truth and diffusers of this pure Love. My life amongst you and Nature has culminated into the beauty of this moment. You have helped me to arrive at this discovery within myself. The Truth has awakened within me, and it is time for me to openly share my Light."

Sophia walks over to the alcove and picks up the lamp of forever burning light. Intuitively, she turns it, so the fire is pointing inward, illuminating the poem from deep within the heart of the alcove. The flame brings forth a warm glow from behind the parchment upon which the poem is written. The Light mystically reveals the symbols Sophia has been pondering since her first day at the cottage. The poem comes to life as it weaves together each symbol with its respective meaning.

She begins:

The Infinite

Reflects

Creation

With the Divine forces of Mother Nature

To evolve spirit and matter

Through all forms of life

In order to reveal the sacred Truth

A magnificent wave of Love surges over them as Sophia explains, "My sweet sages, the best way I can describe this Wisdom, is in my own words.

"As it is above, so it is below…The image of God is Love itself, and this glorious image is reflected as our Universe-- this wondrous ocean of Space. Each one of us, every atom of creation is a sacred drop within this ocean. You, me, the unruly vagrants that surrounded you Rose, the pained voices echoing from the wilderness, each of us and all of us are drops from the same Ocean of Love. Every drop is capable of reflecting the Divine Light because we are one in the same with it. When united, we are an ocean of God's Love, reflected as this Universe we create, through our thoughts, our words, and our actions."

The Elders hearts' fill with varied emotions as they realize their time with Sophia is drawing to a close. The woodland creatures sense the bitter-sweetness moving through the meadow, too. Soon, Sophia will begin the road back home, and leave the Garden of Light. The chatter amongst Mother Nature is anxious, but filled with love and support for Sophia. By sunrise, her journey will resume, guided now by her awakened Light.

CHAPTER SEVENTEEN

The sun is taking its time as it peers over the ridgeline this morning. It seems to be sharing Sophia's reluctance to depart from the spiritual garden. But today, Sophia is starting her journey home.

"Change is part of the wonder of life." is heard upon the morning breeze, as Astar sends her blessings to Sophia and the Elders.

Sophia putters around the kitchen, to prepare the morning tea for her cherished Elders one more time before she leaves. She is still a little tired from the celebration and rejoicing amongst the Elders and the woodland creatures, over the awakening of her inner Light. Everyone joined together in bountiful merriment; you would have thought a coronation of sorts had taken place. In truth, Sophia *has* been gifted by a crown--a crown of Wisdom, which has been entrusted to her by the Universe. The fullness of Love that courses throughout her being can never be wholly expressed by mortal thought. She now holds the keys to the expression of this Wisdom.

As for her Elders, Watchers and Messengers, she forges a special relationship with each one of them. Sophia will always be spiritually connected to these wonderful souls, and this gives her the strength she requires to once again leave the ones she loves so deeply. The time has come to depart from the sanctuary of the Garden of Light, to seek her potential beyond the wilderness.

The Elders enter, one by one. A warm breeze ushers in Naseem as he bids "Brightest of mornings to all."

Dew drops express the beauty of Ama as she appears alongside Naseem, softly welcoming the sun, "May the sweetness of this morning carry with us throughout the day."

The veil that Rose ducks behind each night is once again a beautiful sky-blue, but this time there is a luminous rainbow bounding over the scene. Curious, Sophia walks over and takes a closer look at the new depiction upon the veil. "There's a rainbow on Rose's veil, and it begins right here. It starts at the steps of the cottage in the Garden of Light." As Sophia follows the arc of the rainbow she sees her three great white birds, and a little higher up, above the horizon shines the brightest star of the North. Sophia adores the symbols of her sages then she begins to follow the rainbow's arc.

Just then Rose rustles through the veil with some of her angel-baked goodies and that warm, crinkly smile that could melt chocolate. "Isn't this a lovely morning!" She greets them all with good cheer, as she does every morning.

Sophia helps Rose with her basket of goodies and another small bundle Rose has nestled in the crook of her arm. Setting the items down on top of the kitchen table, Sophia chimes in, "Good morning Rose. I was just exploring the magical scene on your cherished veil. It looks like our cottage and garden are encompassed by a colorful bright rainbow. I was just about to see where the rainbow is heading when you pulled the veil back.

Rose walks back to her precious veil and spreads it out so all can see, being very careful not to expose too much. The scene unfurls the most glorious pair of angel wings as misty clouds hovering just below the sun. Sophia connects with the spirit of her mother as she witnesses the graceful beauty of the angelic wings.

Rose picks up the path of the rainbow where Sophia had been interrupted, "My dear Sophia, this rainbow progresses into the valley below, where it sheds Light upon all who will seek it. Seems like a pretty bright rainbow, if you ask me." Rose professes with her signature giggle.

While viewing the mystic veil, Ama and Naseem silently witness the angel-winged clouds embrace the rainbow then set it free to seek its full potential. Then their attention diverts, wondering why Rose is purposefully protecting one corner of the veil from everyone's view.

As they come together around the breakfast table, Sophia points to the bundle of fabric Rose had carried in with her, "What's this Rose?" Sophia asks as she gingerly unravels the luminescent cloth. Ama recognizes the fabric immediately and is touched by Rose's gift. Naseem notices it too as he looks up to view the missing corner from Rose's sacred veil-- the corner she had been hiding from view. This gesture affirms that Sophia is Rose's chosen one.

Sophia unfolds the cloth, to find the original stone that Rose laid upon her path in the woods, seven years ago. "Is this my stone? Is it the one I placed in the symbol on the door? It granted me access into this cottage of loving sages." She runs and opens the door to see the symbol has changed from its sky-blue hue to a brilliant clear crystal, but the stone is once again missing. "Rose I can't take this, it belongs right here within the symbol. It has been part of your home for the past seven years."

Rose takes the stone from Sophia's delicate hand. She walks back toward the table and wraps the stone back in the luminescent fabric as mystic particles fall from it in a glowing trail, "No, my dear, this stone is yours. It always has been. It's your reminder to stay connected to your guiding Spirit. You will need a little help now and then. Take the stone and this piece of cloth. Keep them both close to you along your journey. There will come a time, when you will know to part with it--when the stone has found its next home." Rose quickly places the stone and cloth into Sophia's small pack and begins to rush her out of the cottage, with the door closing quickly behind her. "You know how I hate long good-byes...besides...I am always with you in spirit. You may visit me as you wish."

It is as if Sophia is twelve years old, in the sweet elder's cottage at the bottom of the hill once again. Rose is rushing her and her belongings out the door with hurried hugs and swift kisses from all. The cottage door shuts with a puff of dust, no giggles this time, just the sniffles of the kindest soul anyone could ever imagine.

Sophia slings her pack onto her back then turns toward the Garden of Light and all the wonderful souls that helped her arrive to this point in time. With joy and grace, Sophia steps forward along her life's journey...high above, three majestic white birds and the guiding star of the North imperceptibly dot the bright blue sky.

As Sophia begins her walk down the trail, making a sweeping arc toward the valley below, she hears Rose's voice of encouragement, "Stay connected to the Spirit of Love, and light the path for others."

CHAPTER EIGHTEEN

The walk down the hill is much different than the journey Sophia made ascending the mountain. It is unusually hot for this time of the morning. She stops to rest on a ledge, hoping to catch a breeze going by. She begins taking in the view, high above the valley. The activity of the city below takes shape as the darkened soot and exhaust of the morning labor rises from the shallow ground. The thick smoky blanket of consumption prevents the weary workers from seeing the Light that shines from within their hearts.

Sophia becomes uneasy as persistent thoughts invade her serenity. She tries to shake them off, one by one, as if they are unwelcome bugs at a summer picnic. She realizes that she is stalling. She doesn't want to face the darkness that exposes itself to her. There's no way around it. The only way home is to walk through the wilderness into the valley, and she must do it alone. No one else can do this for her. She whispers to herself, "I don't want to leave the Garden of Light. Up here, with the Elders, it's all so perfect."

Gently, Rose's voice encourages her along, "Your wisdom must be shared. Go forward; shed Light over all who will turn toward it." Sophia stands up with a sigh of acceptance, and makes her way toward the edge of the woods, bringing the memory of her dear friend, the timber wolf, along for courage.

The deeper she goes into the forest the more uncomfortable she becomes. The heat combined with the stillness in the air is making it difficult to breathe. Sophia stops to rest then she hears the trickles of running water. She follows the sound to a babbling brook that leads to a large pond. As she approaches the water she realizes this is the scene from her day dream. The one she envisioned several years ago while climbing this great mountain. The big boulder, she leaned over to dip her hand into the cool clear waters of the mountain spring is now dead ahead!

Sophia runs over to the boulder, throws down her pack and is ready to drink in some of the cold refreshing water, when she notices the water is not crystal clear at all. The spring is actually a shallow black pond with a dense murky bottom. Rather than risk drinking from it, she decides to dip a scarf into the water and wrap it around her neck to keep herself cool during the remainder of her descent.

She reaches in her pack; the first thing she pulls out is Rose's cloth. Just as she completes the motion of pulling the fabric, her stone falls from its protective folds, into the dark waters. It is as if she is watching it happen in slow motion, yet she can't stop it from falling. She stares at the spot where her treasured stone dropped out of sight. The water rings are repeatedly echoing back to her as if the stone is calling out to be rescued. She looks up to the sky, thinking aloud, "What a stupid move!" As she looks back into the dark waters, she mutters, "How could I have let that happen?" She is hesitant to go in after her stone. Something about the murky water brings fear back into her thoughts.

As the pond water stills, she sees timber wolf's reflection upon the glassy water. His face of courage reminds her to stay connected to her guiding Spirit, and to fear nothing. She hears the words, "Your awakened fire will light your way, do not fear darkness, ever!" With those words, Sophia reaches into the pond. Deeper and deeper she must extend her body into the murk in order to find the muddy bottom. Before she knows it, she is leaning over, upside down, immersed into the waters of the pond all the way over her head, and then she hears them. The pained voices, they are calling out to her again. The wretched noise is coming from beneath the pond waters. She wildly feels around for her stone, it keeps sliding out of her reach as she frantically grasps through the slippery scum. The voices get louder, the deeper she reaches. With one final lunge, she grabs ahold of the stone and repels herself from the bottom of the pond. She scrambles back from the edge and leans against the boulder as she catches her breath. She listens quietly for the voices from the darkness once again, but it is silent. The scum-filled pond is where the secrets await for Sophia.

Just then a faint breeze lifts her delicate veil from the grassy bank and drops it onto the surface of the pond, as it spreads out upon the waters; the pond settles its murk to reveal the crystal waters of her past vision. Carefully, Sophia reaches over and lifts the veil from the surface of the water. As she does, she begins to see images of the individuals that have been calling out to her. Slowly, upon the surface of the still waters, the scenes reveal their hidden stories....

...crying and whimpering comes from a darkened alley, where a woman is begging to be left alone. A heavy set, unshaven man with a grotesquely open wound over his left eyebrow is leaning over her, bellowing his will at her with his putrid breath. He reaches up with a closed fist, ready to unleash his broken past upon the innocence of his new bride! As his intention exposes itself atop the pond, the skies darken above Sophia.

A ripple on the surface of the waters reveals the next scene...a group of native people are standing with their arms linked to each other, chanting their song of sorrow in unison. High above, from her luxurious penthouse office, a tall, needle-nosed executive of a lucrative strip-mining company peers out of her office windows at the hopeful crowd below. Her anger is building at the costly interruption to her valuable business day. Tapping her gold-tipped shoe impatiently, she turns on her designer heels and commands her minions to bid her dirty work. "Strip out this crowd, then strip out their land of every ounce worth selling!" A loud burst of thunder carries those words to each of the tear-covered faces chanting from below.

Another ripple reveals yet another story...two leaders of a nation...divided...one on one side, one on the other... screaming at each other as if raising their voices could raise their understanding of the other. They have mistaken force for faith. Each side battles to impose his will upon the people of the other's side. The battle lines go far and deep. They cross families, neighborhoods, nations and history. The wailing, over the spilling of blood in the name of faith, becomes deafening!

Sophia finds herself crying too, her tears fall heavily into the prophetic pool of water. She looks up to the skies again, as the distant voice of a mystic sage expresses, "Men fight about religion on Earth, in heaven they shall find out that there is only one religion—the worship of God's Spirit." With that, the weighty drops of rain become unleashed by the thunderous clouds above, ushering Sophia back to her path.

The downpour stops as suddenly as it had started. It is still hot and now very muggy. Sophia carefully folds the cool wet fabric and places it around her neck, while keeping a tight grip on her stone. It still gives her the strength to keep her fears at bay.

She picks up her pack and picks up her pace down the hill. The entire way, her mind is reflecting upon the lives of the people revealed by the pond waters. It isn't long before she finds herself on the outer edge of the woods. At the clearing, she is standing on top of the last hill before entering the city below, once again. It's the same hill where she chased her little robin into the forest. She reminisces for a moment as she catches her breath then slowly continues down the path.

Finally, she sees something that brings a smile to her pensive face. Coming into view is the little old cottage where she first met Rose. A fleeting thought, of running in to see if Rose is there, enters then leaves her mind just as quickly. The interruption comes when she notices a young boy--about twelve years old--resting on the very same rock she chose to sit upon so many years ago. Further down the hill Sophia spots a sweet, kind-faced old woman carrying up a heavy load of bags.

The old woman looks up at Sophia for a quick second, gives a crinkly smile and a wink as she makes her way into a group of over-zealous vagrants.

"Oh Rose, so this is how you initiate your students." Sophia laughs out loud as she passes through the scene, without causing any interference, secretly wondering if the young boy will meet the challenge to seek his full potential.

As Sophia completes her descent, a bright rainbow of light follows her into the valley below.

CHAPTER NINETEEN

"Good morning." Roger greets Astar with slight reservation in his voice. He walks over to the coffee pot and gets his first cup of morning brew. "Well, we've done it. The house is completed now. Should we tie a big yellow ribbon around it, or just put it up for sale to the first bidder that walks by?" The stench of his sarcasm hangs in the air like three-day old fish. Even he can't stand what he just said.

Astar snaps back with, "Well, *good morning to you as well!*" hoping to bring Roger's perspective in line with his accomplishment. "The ribbon isn't a bad idea, but no one will be selling this house, oh no, sir. There are big plans for this place…big, big plans, you will see."

Astar makes Roger laugh as he shakes his head with amazement at her ability to turn his demeanor to joy and laughter. No matter what his ailment, she can still fix it. He fills his cup again, and heads out to the front porch to sit on one of the many rockers aligned to face the flower beds and Hope's oak tree.

Today is the first day in three, that the sun manages to poke through the dreary rain clouds surrounding

Hope's Haven. Astar peers out of the kitchen window to the expansive views of the grounds. To her delight, she witnesses a glorious rainbow beginning to form from the Far East hills. She smiles at the beautiful creation as it arches its majestic colors and seems to land right atop the newly built home. "Roger, Roger! Can you see it?" Astar calls out.

The new home is much bigger than the old two-story ranch house at the bottom of the hill. Roger doesn't hear Astar calling out to him, but he too is mesmerized by the massive rainbow and the intensity of its colors. He walks off the porch and enters the gardens, in awe of the scene. Rain is sprinkling down tenderly, as he basks in the full glory of the rainbow. "Astar, come outside, you've got to see this!" The rainbow is engulfing the grounds, as the warmth of the sun kisses every raindrop, releasing their gift of light.

Astar runs out of the front door and into the garden where they both watch as the rainbow seems to follow them around the grounds. The rainbow is chasing their steps with amusement and anticipation. Breathlessly she whispers, "What a spectacular sight!"

Slowly a vision begins to form for Astar. It is a majestic scene of a beautiful woman walking down the arc of the rainbow, bringing many explorers along with her. As Astar connects with the light of this rainbow she declares, "Our darling Sophia is on her way. She is coming home.

"There isn't much time before her arrival. We will soon be having a celebration here. There are lots of preparations to do yet. We better get busy." Astar exclaims as their excitement continues to build.

Roger can't contain his joy when he hears word of Sophia's homecoming. He picks Astar up and swings her around as though she is a rag doll. His laughter echoes down into the valley, awakening the locals to the news.

Over the past few years, the entire town watched from the valley below, while the huge mansion was being built. They observed in wonder as the structure steadily grew, took form, and over time adorned the green hilltop with its magnificent, white splendor. Many of them visited during the construction and found themselves with hammer in hand, shooting the breeze with Roger, as they willfully helped bring the home into fruition.

While the structure is quiet large, with accommodations for many souls, it rests peacefully within the curves of the hills. The native tribal council helped design and build the home to complement its surroundings and take advantage of the healing energies of the land.

As Roger and Astar continue to view the gorgeous rainbow that is enlivening the grounds, the tribal elder comes walking up the path to the home. "Roger, your home receives the blessing. It is a home of peace, for the rainbow blesses it with beauty, love and enlightenment. Soon you will open the heart of this home to all those who seek to understand their deepest truth." A smile of approval adorns the dark wrinkles of his face. "This home will honor our sacred land."

With those words, he sits cross legged, in the middle of the rain-soaked grass, in front of the house. He takes a small hand-carved flute from inside his leather pouch and begins to play a melody in honor of the peace, love and light that is surrounding them.

This makes Roger profoundly happy. While it is true that Roger inherited this land from his family, he has always respected the history of the land. He sees himself as a steward rather than owner, which makes the blessing of the tribal council a welcome sign.

"Roger you must invite the town to visit the grounds. We are gathering to welcome this rainbow light...she is coming home. This will be a sanctuary for peace. All will come together in harmony, just as the colors of the rainbow unite here today." The tribal elder is pleased.

CHAPTER TWENTY

The lights of the town begin to glow as dusk settles in for the evening. Sophia needs to find a place to rest tonight before boarding the ship in the morning. But her thoughts are with the voices. "Who are these people? Where can I find them? What can I do, even if I do find them? Who am I to offer them help?" She is caught in a frenzy of questions. The battle lines of fear and love begin taking shape as she thinks of the voices and visualizes the individuals that call out to her.

While deep in thought, she continues walking down a darkened alley, where she finds an inn, not too far from the docks. Sophia enters and waits by the front desk for assistance. As she looks around, she notices that everything is meticulously clean, but in an unnerving manner. *Nothing* is out of place, no dust to be found anywhere...all the fire wood is stacked neatly by the hearth...even the fringe of the carpet has been combed to stand at attention. Something is off, out of balance and uneasy about this place.

Sophia feels the tiny hairs on the back of her neck stand up straight as she hears a man's voice bark out commands,

"Someone's out front! Get out there...now! What are ya' waitin' for? Do I have to do everythin' for ya'?!"

Sophia has only been waiting a few seconds, before a beautiful young woman, not much older than herself, timidly greets her, "Ev'nin' Miss, how can I help you?" She hangs her head low, coercing her beautiful flowing hair to cover her face.

Unexpectedly, the scent of Hope enters the room as a soft breeze brushes away the woman's tousled locks. Her secret is exposed momentarily, long enough for Sophia to hear her mother's voice whisper, "Truth is One; perspectives are many. Seek Truth!" The woman suddenly looks up as if she too heard the secret message on the breeze.

When their eyes connect, Sophia sees the purple and green hues surrounding the woman's face and the bruised hand print carelessly left around her dainty neck. Quickly she lowers her head in shame and wipes away a solitary tear that dared to show itself. Although the room is still of any sounds, Sophia can sense the woman silently begging to be saved from this personal pit of darkness.

Sophia reaches over and lays her hand compassionately upon the woman's trembling fingers. While looking her straight in the eyes, she quietly but resolutely whispers, "First thing in the morning, I am boarding the ship from the West; heading to a sanctuary of peace nestled in a haven of hope." Then she states for *all* to hear, "I will only need a room for one night."

The woman pulls her hand away uneasily as her emotions begin unraveling like the stiches of a woolen sweater being pulled apart. "Yes, Miss...um, I'll get you set up, right away..." she fumbles over her words. She fidgets with some papers atop the counter while attempting to gain control of her fears. She is trying to compose herself from the shocking kindness she has just received, from a perfect stranger. It makes her uncomfortable. She just wants to be left alone to tend to her list of chores when, from the kitchen, a sudden cough then violent thrashing is heard.

The woman hurries back to find her husband choking, on the chicken dinner he had been stuffing into his gullet, between shouting orders to his wife. At first she hesitates, then runs over to aid him. In his distress, he grabs her wrist tightly in a panicked demand for help. She struggles to get free to be able to assist him, but his fear is more powerful than the both of them.

Sophia enters the kitchen upon hearing the commotion. There she finds him, with eyes bulging in a desperate attempt to inhale one freeing breath. As Sophia gets closer, she sees it--the oozing open wound over his left eyebrow. "You!" She says under her breath with disgust as she battles the urge to let him choke, just as he had choked the freedom out of his young wife. But Sophia's will begins to be guided by the Light within. She sees the ☥ symbol, sent by her sages, as it faintly hovers above his convulsing body. With one bold and sweeping move, Sophia punches the man square in his gut, displacing an entire chicken thigh from his throat, in one foul swoop.

Sophia catches a glimpse of the battered woman standing a little taller, and taking in a small breath of freedom just as the punch lands, only to be imprisoned again by his wretched voice.

"Ugh, jeezuz that hurt like a sonnuvabitch!" is all he can muster as 'gratitude'. His voice is raw and scratchy, but unmistakable, as he moans, "Get me some whiskey! I need my whiskey!!" His fat fist slams the table hard enough to rattle the grease-covered silverware.

"You're welcome." Sophia says with a hint of sarcasm, as she straightens up to look at the man behind the wound. Her harsh judgment of him gives way to empathy as she begins to seek truth. Her understanding of this man is slowly developing. His many years of abuse and abandonment emerge through Sophia's visions, revealing how he acquired that jagged wound above his distant stare. She begins to see the cycle of his past. She witnesses how this history continues into his present days and nights of punishment. Deliberately, he picks at the scar; he will not allow the wound to heal.

"Move outta the sunlight, so I can see ya!" he commands Sophia, as he nervously picks at the open wound with one hand, while pouring himself a generous glass of whiskey with the other. The whiskey has become his savior over the years, bringing on a coveted bout of amnesia each night.

Of course, Sophia is not standing in the sunlight, for the evening winds already lace the night sky with clusters of stars. Clearly, something else is happening. Her aura is so bright for his darkened existence that he cannot bear to look directly at her.

As he leans back to spill his precious whiskey into his thirsting mouth, he gruffly adds, "Your punch musta packed a whollup missy, cuz I can see a rainbow of light coming outta yer--"

His words are like a bolt of lightning, flashing the truth of the moment into Sophia's heart. Undoubtedly, *his* voice belongs to one of the trapped souls calling to her from the wilderness. Before he can finish his sentence, she walks over to him and places her hands over his eyes, covering the open and infected wound, too. He jerks his head away, but his reluctance caves to her compelling aura. Her touch brings a sense of calm that he has not experienced, but he longs for, in stolen moments from time to time.

Sophia takes a deep, cleansing breath as she once again hears the distant voice of a mystic sage, guiding her to understand the truth of this man, "The real person does not consist solely of what is seen at any particular moment, but is composed of the sum of all its various and changing conditions, from its appearance in the material form, to its disappearance from earth."

"I understand." Sophia responds aloud to the Elder's gift, while the man hears those two simple words spoken to *him* for the first time in his life.

She continues to cover his eyes with her hands, enabling him to reflect upon the reality he helped to create up till now. By the Light of Truth, she guides him through his own thoughts, words and actions of the past. He doesn't need to reach back too far into his bank of deeds before seeing his beleaguered wife, for the first time with a sober view. He observes himself beating the innocence and beauty out of her sacred life. He is frightened by his actions. He has become one with the vile offenders of his own hidden past. Tears fall from his eyes as he sees himself in the intensity of this Light. He feels the Light washing over him, healing the diseases and dis-eases of his past. This cleansing allows him to seek another way of being...the Light begins to shine from within him...showing him the potential of life.

Sophia's healing touch is bringing new images to this man, allowing him to glimpse his future. Images of a life filled with love, gentleness and nurturing begin to form. He attempts to fight the vision at first, thinking he does not deserve this, but Love surrounds him. It is as if Sophia is raising this man up from his own dark past with the conveyance of Light and Love.

He drops to his knees in gratitude for the clarity he receives through Sophia. He looks up at her, seeking guidance for his future. As she looks upon him, she momentarily sees the essence of her timber wolf enter his presence, giving him the courage to begin seeking his true potential. She unlocks the Spirit of Love from within the hardened clutches of his past. Light shows him how to soften his heart to allow Love to breathe and grow from within.

He stands and walks over to his wife, who is unaffected by the Light *he* sees. She cowers down in his shadow, preparing herself for his usual but unwelcome greeting. But it does not come. What used to be the putrid stench, of his hurtful words, no longer lingers on the air she breathes. The energy has shifted. The tension has melted away and a gentle man stands before her in this moment. She lifts her bruised face to meet his, eye to eye. He risks raising his hand toward her, this time to softly brush back her hair. They both begin to cry when they imagine what the future could hold. Between his tears he takes time to acknowledge his wrongs and apologize for his actions. Then he does something that neither of them expects, he asks for forgiveness.

She waits, stunned and motionless, just like a bird that has been held in a tiny cage for years then is at once set free. She doesn't quite know if it is safe to soar. Soon enough, she collects her wits and a few belongings before she flies out the door, without a spoken word.

CHAPTER TWENTY-ONE

The sun's rays pour through the open window onto the grease stains of his t-shirt. His round belly is exposed to the intense light. He looks like a pillow placed in the sunlight to be 'disinfected', just like his stepmother used to do. He slowly comes to, awakening to the light, once again.

"Miss, is that you?" he beckons, leaning forward, "Hey Missy? Are ya' there?" He asks again, in hopes of hearing Sophia's healing voice in response. But it dawns on him; the bright light he sees now *is* the morning sun. He had fallen asleep at the kitchen table where his life unexpectedly changed course the night before. He is not accustomed to being awakened by sunlight. One of his wife's nightly chores had been to close all the windows and shutters. He didn't want to allow the light in, or their secrets out!

As the sun shines upon his surroundings, he sees clearly that he is on his own. He looks around for any sign of the woman who released him from his fearful existence. She was his guiding light, but now she's gone. Without her support, he feels fear creeping into his newborn freedom. "She's gone? She just leaves me here, abandoned, without hope?" He begins to feel the panic rising around him again like a drowning man in a stormy sea.

Then, he hears the front door creak open. He rushes out to greet Sophia, and to pick up where they left off. He pulls open the door and joyfully shouts, "You've come back!"

To his surprise and dismay, it is his young wife. She sees the disappointment in his face, but she notices something else--his wound. For the first time the festering wound over his eye is healing. The energy shift she felt the night before is still present within the home, but her sense of self-preservation keeps screaming at her to turn and run.

He confesses, "I'm sorry. I just thought that you wuz the lady from last night. I wuz jus' hopin' that she came back to help me. She showed me a new way to live, but now she's gone." He walks over to the living room table where he notices an envelope with hand writing upon it—"Seek Truth". Inside is payment for one night's stay, and a hand-written note that expands the message, "Seek Truth and you will find your potential!" Nothing else is written--no name, no address-- nothing. He feels lost without her light to guide him. He falls back onto the sofa, feeling abandoned yet again.

At that moment, his wife grabs the note from his trembling hand and scribbles something on it. Then she crumples the note into his fist and utters, "This is the best I can do with regards to forgiving you right now. I hope you understand. You can check the evening registry for her name." With those words, she turns and walks out of the door, leaving their past behind.

He loosens his grip on the note. Inside the paper is the frail wedding band he placed on her finger just a few months ago. The golden band glimmers to reveal a more valuable detail beneath it. His wife has written out the words Sophia whispered to her the night before. In a hasty script she wrote, "She's boarding the ship from the West, going to a peace sanctuary at hope's haven." His departing wife left him with all that he needs to begin his search for truth.

CHAPTER TWENTY-TWO

The sea mist is rising up and surrounding the ship in the early morning hours of dawn. "She's impressive, isn't she?" Sophia says, looking up at the mighty vessel, as she mingles with the crowd of passengers beginning to line up on the wooden dock. "She's the same old girl, that's for sure!" Sophia exclaims as she reads, 'BEATRIX' in bold black letters on the ship's bow. A fresh coat of snow-white paint elegantly adorns her massive steel outlines as she welcomes her passengers aboard.

The wait is long to get onboard, but once Sophia reaches the top of the gangway, she heads toward the back of the ship. From this vantage point she bids farewell to the mountain she called home for the past seven years. The peaceful summit stands quietly in the background of the rising sun, as its secret inhabitants preserve the most sacred of treasures. "I am eternally grateful to you for showing me the way home." She whispers softly upon the mystic winds to her sages, messengers and guides, and then gives a special wink to the skies for her dearest companion, the timber wolf, whose spirit is loyally by her side.

Her parting thoughts are interrupted by the ship's horn blast before Beatrix slowly surges away from her berth. Sophia glances amongst the waves of people that are now crowding the docks to bid their loved ones "bon voyage". She looks for one particular soul while quietly wondering if her hand-written note has yet been discovered. When he is not found, she allows her disappointment to wane in the wake left behind the ship as she pulls away from the dock.

After a short while, the ship clears the boundaries of the harbor permitting the Captain to command her engines to pick up speed. The loud snapping sound of the ship's flag battling against the wind captures Sophia's attention. She leans against the cold metal railing, as the ship lurches ahead. The massive flag of the West flies proudly in honor of the ship's home port. Looking up at the fluttering banner, Sophia proclaims aloud, "Home, I'm going home!" She embraces the fullness of those words, as sweet memories of home fill her thoughts.

As Sophia thinks of home, she envisions her father's creation. She imagines the beautiful white mansion, sitting high in the hills. It is majestic, yet serene. Its peaceful beauty is enhanced by the mist that surrounds the hilltop as if the home sits upon the clouds. Leading up to the home, is a long gravel road with a wrought-iron sign at the base of the road that reads, "Hope's Haven". As one follows the gravel road up toward the mansion there is a garden gate, surrounding soft green grass, and sweet smelling roses, and in the front corner of the garden there is a beautiful weeping willow tree that dances with the breezes. Inside the gate is a dirt path that leads to a beautiful wooden porch. The porch is deep and long, and it wraps around the entire home. She spots her father sitting amongst a row of rocking chairs that are aligned to face her mother's lovely oak tree; with a panoramic view of the gardens and the valley below.

Sophia glimpses her dad etching upon large stone disks, but she can't quite see what he's making. "I guess he must not be finished with it yet", she mumbles to herself, as she sees him set one stone disk down to the right of his chair, while he struggles to pick up the last disk from his stack.

Then she envisions Astar, upstairs, choosing the perfect placement for flower vases and healing crystals. She's in a room that has views of the entire valley, which is glorious from this outlook. There is so much to discover, Sophia can't wait to see all the marvels of her father's creation. Soon she will be home.

The rhythm of the waves beating against the hull brings Sophia's devotion back to her journey as Beatrix propels across the depths of the ocean. The command for "more power" is once again given. The ship shudders then heaves ahead, reluctantly.

Beneath the layers of paint, that cover her immense façade, rests the oxidized truth of years of dedicated service crossing these salty seas. This vessel works hard, but keeps her age disguised to elude that one inevitable voyage. Beatrix shudders again, the sound of her fear bellows from the bowels of her engine room as she strains to make her destination.

Above deck the breeze is cool and steady even though the glide of the ship is not. Sophia watches the homeland of her sages disappear into the deep blue ocean as mysteriously as it had revealed itself long ago. With a sigh, she decides it's time to settle in for the duration of her trip.

After asking for a little direction to her accommodations, she finds herself on top deck as she opens the door to her cabin. The Elders surprised Sophia with a beautiful stateroom that sits high above the restless waves. From this perch, Sophia can at once ponder where she came from and to where she is heading along her voyage.

CHAPTER TWENTY-THREE

Every morning while at sea, Sophia goes down to the lowest deck of the ship, to be close to the sea as she witnesses the rising sun of the East. The glorious golden disk emerges from the ocean depths slowly revealing the blurred line between heaven and earth. Sophia softly graces each morning with blessings of love. She offers her gratitude and joy for another wonder-filled day and then walks back to her cabin to prepare for breakfast.

On this day, she hears the buzzing of rumors and stories being whispered amongst the passengers as they slowly begin to awaken and gather around the decks. Sophia asks a group gathering by the ship's railing, "What's happening? Why is everyone out so early this morning?"

A young man offers her a folded note which is on official ship stationary, it reads: "Due to unforeseen circumstances, we must make an unscheduled stop. All passengers will be disembarking at Noon, boarding our sister ship, ANASTASIA for departure by 6:00PM." She returns the note with a "thank you" and quickly heads to her cabin to pack.

On the way to her cabin, the ship tremors yet again in the deep waters, rattling the passengers as she flounders at sea. Her power has been diminished since her prime so many years ago. Beatrix winces on, toward the sliver of land that is appearing upon the horizon. Her engines are struggling.

Just then, Sophia is drawn to another voice from the wilderness. It comes quietly, yet full of sorrow. She doesn't yet know to whom the voice belongs, as the image connected with it stays in the dark waters of the pond. "There it is again." She exclaims as she hears the muffled calls. The voice belongs to a man adrift at sea; he is calling for help, for he believes himself to be lost. His voice is tired and ready to give up, but his soul is calling for guidance.

She questions herself. "Has someone gone overboard? Should I be looking in the waters?" Then her intuition gives her the guidance she requests. Sophia follows the distinct voice, the sound of his desperate calls; she follows it all the way to the door of the Captain's helm. She is pulled in to meet the Captain, for it is *his* voice that calls out for help. Upon entering she finds him leaning against a weathered wooden stool, sipping cold coffee and mulling over tattered schematics of the ship's engines. He is focusing on finding a way to extend his ship's time at this final hour, but the cycle of life is inescapable. The Laws of Nature keep whirling ahead, just as the symbol of the fiery cross of Nature , makes its presence known within Sophia's line of sight. The image hovers above the Captain's head, informing Sophia of this man and his plea.

The Captain is tall and gaunt for he has withered down from the hearty physic of his youth. The many years of sunshine and salt air have crafted a leathery yet amiable smile on the old mariner. He looks up from the dated papers and unfurls his troubled brow as Sophia enters. Her aura brightens the room and his darkened thoughts in the same moment. With one look into his sunken brown eyes, Sophia understands his calls of distress. Beatrix--his ship, this mariner's life--has been his one true passion. He has captained her since her maiden voyage, almost thirty years ago.

The Captain rises to greet Sophia, but his anguish, for the outcome of his ship, cannot be hidden behind the gentleness of his voice. "How can I help you, young lady?" His voice softly cracks, as he chokes back his fear of loss.

Upon hearing the Captain's voice, the Light within her brightens, "Good morning Captain. My name is Sophia Cahill; I'm one of your passengers. I'm sorry to interrupt your work sir, but I want to thank you for this voyage, she's been a gracious host. Beatrix, that is." Sophia can sense the Captain's grief. He is about to lose Beatrix, the only meaningful part of his life, up till now. This will be the ship's last port before she meets her end. He thought he could delay the unavoidable, but time was not on their side. Sophia can see the final moments as Beatrix struggles to cut through the deep water.

The Captain peers out of the window to the few anxious tugboats heading toward them. As each tug draws closer, his heart tightens with fear. "I am nothing without this ship." He quietly confesses, to the Light he sees beaming from Sophia's kindness.

"That is not your truth." Sophia states, as a matter of fact. Her words enter his heart and mind with authority and love in the same instance.

"She's the lighthouse in the storm," he thinks, as he reveals the darkness within his heart to her. He sits back down on his wooden stool, and in a tone of submission, he recounts what will become of his ship. "Within a matter of weeks, this mighty vessel will go through the most undeserving of burials. Once they beach her bow onto shore, she will be shackled and drawn by heavy machinery completely out of her watery home. The scavengers will devour her of any vestige of her majestic past. What is left will be ripped apart and sold as scrap." He mourns her coming death, as he watches silently out of the window. The tugboats are surrounding them.

Sophia attempts to soften the Captain's fear, "It is never about how one dies, but how one *lives*! Captain, you have guided her well. She's had many honorable years even more than you had imagined. The truth is that Beatrix will become a spiritual voyager. Soon she will journey in the memory of all whom she has touched. The stories, friends and families that shared their experiences with her, will live on...her spirit will forever be carried within you too, for we are all connected.

Beatrix now surrenders her power. She lies still in the waters near the coast. The powerful tugs tie her down with their heavy ropes and bind her to their overbearing will, as they tow the timeworn vessel into the harbor. She lists to one side as they push her against the dock. Her propellers give a residual groan before they are stilled. She won't be here for long. Her stay is temporary, just long enough to unload her cargo and passengers. In due time, she will be towed into the tide.

Sophia continues, "The vessel dies, but the Spirit lives on." She lays her hand upon the Captain's, reassuring his soul. Through Sophia's connection with the Light, the Captain sees his future.

His mind fills with refreshed thoughts, as he imagines himself on a different type of voyage. Sophia continues to hold his hand as the Captain maps his new bearings by the Light that shines around him. He can feel the flicker of his own flame ignite, as the images of possibilities lift his heart.

"Miss Cahill, is it? Don't think me an old fool, but I see a rainbow of light around you young lady. Why, it's like you're a walking lighthouse. I can see this light glowing around you just as clearly as I watched the sunrise this morning!" The Captain is bewildered, yet welcoming of every image and emotion that is being stirred within him. "I have been lost for the past few years, while I've been working to hide my vessel's failing condition. I thought my life would most assuredly be over if I had to leave Beatrix. So I lied, and covered up her ailments, just so I could cheat time." He shakes his head, seeing his own foolishness. "Time moves forward, no one can stop it. It's a law of Nature, isn't it?

"But you know what? Up until the moment you walked into my helm, I was looking for a loophole, a way around these laws of time and Nature. What a fool, I've been." As the Light shines truth before him, he discovers more within himself. "It's funny, I can't really explain what you've done here, but I feel a tremendous sense of calm." He chuckles silently, then with full acceptance of his new awakening, he states aloud, "You're my lighthouse in this storm."

Sophia comforts the Captain, "This is not the end of your journey, sir. Your voyage will continue, but with a new and differing compass heading. You're right. These are the laws of Nature; her cycle of creation, growth and dissolution, only to be created yet again."

The Captain is deeply moved by Sophia's compassionate understanding and gentle guidance. It is true he is losing Beatrix, but he is finding his true potential. "I understand that while I have dedicated my life to the honor and steel of this wonderful ship, my new journey will be led by my soul. You have lit a pathway that I have always kept hidden from myself in the past. You have helped me reconnect with the fire inside of me. I want to learn about my soul's journey, and what my true potential could be."

The Captain's energy is enlivened with a thirst for knowledge. His heart receives the Spirit of Love. Light awakens the Love within his soul.

CHAPTER TWENTY-FOUR

Sophia runs back to her cabin to quickly pack her belongings. When she lays everything on the bed she notices something extraordinary about her veil. A golden fringe is present all the way around the square cut cloth. The veil has grown. When Sophia takes a closer look, she sees two bands of expansion around her precious veil. "What the heck is going on with this?" She holds it up to the sunlight to get a clearer view. "This is stunning." As the veil moves into the light, golden specs of dust fall from its new edges. Sophia runs her hand beneath the falling speckles, playfully inquiring aloud, "Rose, is this your handiwork?" The shimmer is beautiful, but the question remains unanswered. "How did these bands of growth appear?"

Her querying mind is interrupted by a loud knock on the cabin door, "All ashore!" The call to disembark is becoming urgent. Sophia moves quickly to pack, but the veil no longer fits into her small sack. Hurriedly, she wraps the veil around her shoulders, to keep it safely nearby. She then places her treasured stone into her shirt pocket, close to her heart. Once again the loud rap on the door is heard, followed by, "All ashore!!"

The decks are crowded with passengers and luggage as people make their way off the ship. Most are already on queue to board the Anastasia, quickly forgetting their prior home at sea, as they leave Beatrix behind in her final hours. The lines are growing long and the mid-morning sun is beaming down upon the impatient crowd.

Sophia decides to forego the lines and venture around the city, knowing she has several hours before the Anastasia will be set free upon the seas. She throws her small pack onto her back and lets her curious nature lead the way. As she walks away from the hectic harbor, she is guided downtown, to city center. Turning the corner onto a beautiful, tree-lined boulevard she begins to hear the steady beating of drums. The drum beats fall in unison with the rhythm of Sophia's heart.

As she approaches the corner, she nears the large crowd that is gathering at the intersection. Everyone is drawn to the chanting that can now be heard in harmony with the beat of the drums. Sophia keeps moving ahead till she can make her way to an opening in the crowd.

Right in front of her, she recognizes the scene—the chanting people, arms linked together, rocking from side to side in one unified circle. They are raising their voices to the sky. Once again, the images and voices from the wilderness materialize by the Light in her path.

An old, yet hopeful, indigenous soul approaches Sophia with this greeting, "Rainbow warrior, you have come. I am Chief Rongomau. My people have been calling to the skies for the Power to shine its Wisdom, and now you are here. I can see your bright rainbow!"

Sophia quickly understands the plight of his people as their leader conveys his thoughts to her, telepathically. The Natives gather here, around this building, in hopes to speak to the leaders of the company that occupies their land. The executive lust for gain perpetuates the strip-mining of land beneath their sea. They foresee the damage that is coming-- healthy beds of coral, kelp and sea life will be displaced, churned and dumped as refuse upon the ocean floor, dimming all hope for renewal of the sea for many generations to come. Fishing rights and territories that are centuries old will be destroyed, all in the name of profit, but at what cost?

Sophia steps closer to the wise one saying, "I understand the problem, but how can I help? I have no connection with this company. I have no path to influence a change within the hearts and minds of the executives who make these decisions."

The old leader gives her a toothless smile. He raises his right hand to the sun then points to Sophia's shirt pocket. Then he raises his left hand to the company's sign on the side of the building then once again points to Sophia's shirt pocket. He clasps his hands together in prayer and kneels down to wait for answers.

Touched by his cause, she lays her right hand upon his head and beckons him to rise up. She lifts the elder up and promises to meet with the executives who are in charge. "I will do my best to voice your peoples' concerns."

She turns to face the building, looking up to the penthouse offices that seem to pierce the skies. As she makes her way to the entry, she stops dead in her tracks upon seeing the logo above the entrance. "I can almost hear the tapping of her gold-tipped shoes," she blurts out while remembering the image of the woman executive upon the pond waters. She looks back at the elder, turns toward the sign once again to make sure she's not mistaken in what she sees and then bolts for the elevator, impatiently waiting its arrival. When the doors wisp open, a lanky, pimple-faced teen asks in a bored tone of voice, "What floor?"

Sophia calls out, "Penthouse…Infinity Mining…take me to the Penthouse." She grabs her stone from her pocket and compares the symbol on it to the symbol on the company's logogram atop the plaque in the elevator. It's identical. The person, she is rushing to meet, is an executive of ∞ Infinity Mining Company!

Her mind is full of questions, but they all come down to one, as she asks with discontent, "How could a symbol honoring such great love be used to represent a company that has turned its back on so many people?" She is eager to get some answers. The excitement has gotten her feverish. She takes off the veil she had fashioned into a shawl, and places the stone into the folds of the veil. When the two unite, they bring forth a sense of focus and composure to Sophia. She breathes deep to gather her thoughts, then centers herself in the task at hand.

Finally the elevator reaches the lofty heights of the Penthouse offices. As the doors sweep open, ∞ INFINITY MINING COMPANY, in big bold letters, is prominently displayed in the foyer. Sophia walks straight into the imposing reception area, where she notices that the receptionist is away from her post. Without pause, she keeps walking past the reception desk to search for the executive offices. She calls forth the image over the pond waters, in order to find the office belonging to this powerful woman. She   revisits the image while talking to herself, "Corner office….large floor to ceiling windows…skinny, tall woman." Sophia keeps walking with authority, as though she belongs on this floor, until she comes upon a pair of huge hand-etched crystal doors with the name, *Claire des Tenebres*, President and CEO written proudly alongside the entrance to the private office. "This has to be it." She reads the name again, "Claire des Tenebres".

Naseem's voice enters Sophia's thoughts urging her, "Connect with her name, my dear Sophia."

Suddenly his guidance is interrupted by the sound of people coming down the hallway toward her. Sophia hastily opens the door to Miss des Tenebres' office and sneaks into the voluminous space.

She turns to view her surroundings as she is greeted by a condescending tone of voice asking, "Are you lost?" The disdain is coming from the woman who recently received her title of 'CEO' from her ailing father.

She is tall, thin and very precise. Each strand of her blond hair, which is woven into a tight bun and balanced atop her head, would attest to that. She is also very attractive, but her demeanor is hiding her true beauty. As she stands there, leaning against the floor to ceiling glass, she's angry. Her resentment over the growing crowd below has been rudely interrupted by Sophia's uninvited appearance. She coldly states, "Clearly you don't work here." She glares at Sophia's attire, giving her the 'once over' from the end of her superior nose. "Why don't you state how you managed to get past reception and into my *private* office, before security shows up and we all miss hearing how your little adventure ends?!" She quips as she is reaching for the phone.

"Wait!" Sophia stalls. She wants to choose her words carefully as she releases her grip on the door handle and walks deeper into the snare. She approaches Claire, but stops suddenly as something peculiar begins to happen with her stone. It is heating up and vibrating violently in her hand. The stone is getting hotter with each step as Sophia moves closer to the incensed CEO. Even the veil does not stop the burning heat that is emanating from the stone as it becomes too hot to withstand. Sophia drops the stone; it rolls on the floor and stops with a loud thud against the heel of Miss Des Tenebres' designer shoe.

The CEO glares down with contempt. "You dropped something," she coldly states as she bends over to pick it up.

"No, wait, it's mine. I'm sorry. It got away from me." Sophia calls out, racing over to reach her precious stone before it falls into the wrong hands.

Claire scoops up the impish little rock, and smugly comments, "Did it? Get away from you?"

"Yes…it has a mind of its own, at times," Sophia grumbles from between her pursed lips, disappointed that she was not able to restrain her stone before its mischievous leap of faith.

Claire begins to taunt Sophia by flipping the stone, like an old coin, into the air. "So, tell me, what's so special about this little rock, hmm? There's a hundred more, just like it, in the planter outside my door. Grab one on your way out!" She barks giving the stone one final flip into the air. As the stone reaches its highest peak and stalls in mid-air, the symbol turns to catch the sun's ray. It reflects the wisdom of the symbol, calming the tension that had built up between the two women.

Sophia watches the spark of wisdom ignite in Claire the moment she connects with the sunlit symbol. A childlike purity comes over Claire's countenance as she cradles the stone in both her hands, saving it from hitting bottom once again. Staring at the symbol resting in her cupped hands, she gently asks, "This symbol, I know it. It's mine. Where did you get this stone?" Claire's youthful innocence has momentarily broken through her pompous mannerisms.

Sophia is moved by the intense wonder that has softened Claire's harsh edges, yet she walks over to retrieve her treasure. As both their hands grab for the stone, the veil wraps itself around the two women and the stone, at once uniting the three and connecting them to their past. Claire, the stone, and Sophia are bound together as one. The whispers of knowledge, understanding and Wisdom begin to emanate, encouraging their souls to seek Truth.

The energy amongst the three of them brightens Sophia's aura. She begins to receive the images of Claire's life as though she is viewing an old family photo album. First, she is shown a snapshot of a strong, young naval officer and his demure wife. They are holding their newborn baby girl, as they proudly stand in front of his ship, in a deep bay, somewhere in Crete.

Next, a picture of a toddler, dressed up as a little cowgirl for Halloween, sitting on her daddy's knee, beneath a sign that reads, 'Port of Haifa, U.S. Naval Base'. Another shot shows a wiry, six year old girl, celebrating her birthday with her schoolmates on the naval base at Naples, Italy.

The veil still binds the stone between them, as it shimmers down spirited particles to reveal an image of a curious, twelve year old adventurer. This explorer comes to life amidst the mystical golden sparkles falling from the veil, setting to motion the past, in their presence.

"That's me! I'm twelve." Claire squeals as if she is taken back to that very moment in time. "I wandered away from the port that day, leaving all that I knew behind. I became curious about three white birds that kept circling over my head. They would call to me and coax me to follow them. So, I chased those birds. I chased them up the hill, to the edge of the woods. I almost caught them too!"

Claire begins spilling details from this encounter that she had not acknowledged before now. "I'm chasing these birds up the hill. I know I should not stray away from the port, my father, 'Rear Admiral Des Tenebres', will kill me! But, I follow the great white birds up to a small cottage, where I stop to catch my breath. There I am. I'm sitting upon a large boulder in front of the cottage. My elbows are resting on my knees as I glance down between my feet. Then, I see this same exact stone!" she lifts the stone up in her hand, bringing Sophia and the entwined veil along on the memory. "I pick up the stone and immediately I feel a sense of warmth surrounding me as if I was receiving a hug from the heavens. Don't ask me to explain it, I can't."

"I understand." Sophia softly encourages, not wanting to break Claire's momentum.

Claire continues with her childhood memory, "The stone feels at home in my hand. But as I'm admiring my new trinket, I hear a raucous. When I look up, I see an old woman being tussled around for a few bags of groceries. I'm compelled to help her, I scream to the aggressors to stop, but they don't. I become frightened...for her...for myself. I yell again from a safe distance. When they don't stop I begin to move closer. As I approach them, I trip over a long stick. For a quick moment I think to use the stick to attack the crowd, but fear awakens the coward inside me, I turn and run back down the hill, to the safety of the port and my father's tall shadow. I'm on the run, down the hill I speed in a frightened frenzy. I must have lost this stone along the way, but the symbol has stayed with me ever since."

Claire is visibly drained from the memory. She falls to her knees as the veil unravels, releasing the truth into the Universe.

She hangs her head in deep disappointment with herself, believing she turned her back on a moment of greatness, when she turned her back on the frail elder. "I ran away. How could I leave that sweet old woman to fend for herself? Who does that?!" While grasping the sacred stone in her tight grip, she questions her past actions and intentions.

Sophia gently rests her hand upon Claire's golden locks that have now broken free from the taut bun, and flow softly around her face. Sophia quietly watches, as Claire peels away the last bit of armor she uses to protect herself in this world of profit and greed.

Sophia's aura encourages on, "Claire, you have never completely turned your back. You have kept this symbol close to you for a reason. When your father started this mining company, so many years ago, you fought to have this symbol represent it. Didn't you? It took courage for you, as a young girl, to stand up to him and express your thoughts. A fire was lit up from deep within you that day, as you pled your case to your father. He could not resist the brightness that was shining from your beaming smile as you spoke of the symbol and its importance to you. This flame has been within you always, but you have not allowed your inner self to connect with it." Sophia lifts Claire's chin along with her spirit before the chanting from the crowd below recaptures the CEO's attention.

Sophia fights to regain Claire's focus. "It wasn't your time then…but it is now. Can you hear them calling to you?"

Claire feels the bristle of irritation creep in, "Yes, I've been listening to them all morning. It has been driving me crazy."

"You've heard the *noise*, but now hear the voices of their souls. It's your time. You're being called now, because you have the power you did not have at the age of twelve. The Universe guided your prosperity to allow you to grow and gain the ability to help more than just one. Your path led you to this moment." Sophia urges Claire to view the faces chanting from below. "They need you now; will you turn your back, or extend your hand?"

"I hear them, I do. But, what am I to do, turn my back on the shareholders, the directors, my father, who has entrusted me to follow in his footsteps?!" Claire is finding it difficult to guide her spirit through the material world she has amassed. But Sophia witnesses love surrounding Claire. An image of Ama suspending the symbol of the double triangles of Spirit and Matter ∇ above Claire brightens into existence, as Claire ponders her choices.

Sophia keeps dropping bread crumbs of wisdom for Claire to find her way to the Light that is beckoning to be awakened from deep within. "Up until this very moment, you have been walking in the shadow of your father's footsteps. All the decisions you have made within your lifetime have led you to right *now*. Truth lives in the *present;* it lives in this moment, and what you choose to do with it."

By now the crowd of on-lookers at the base of ∞ Infinity Mining Company has grown around the entire city block. Strangers join in, raising their voices with the native people of the land. The sound swirls up the steel girders of the building. The energy enters Claire's being, stoking her internal flame as she feels the battle brewing within her. Her face reddens, and her body trembles as if she is about to explode with violence. The unwelcome noise is becoming deafening to Claire as her internal war wages on. She reaches for the phone to call her minions in to do her dirty work. When she leans over her desk, she glimpses the reflection of the spirit-filled symbol, ▽ that has come to be in her presence. The struggle of love and fear--spirit over matter--intensifies as Claire fights to return her focus to dialing the numbers, frantically. She carries the phone over to the window, once again peering down at the chanting crowd. The noise is over whelming as she begins to hear the message behind each voice. Speaking into the phone, Claire begins her commands, "Go into that crowd, find their leader, and bring him back to me, at once!" She slams the phone down and declares, "There's only one way to stop the noise."

Sophia's determination emboldens. "Claire, I've seen the symbol awaken the flame in your heart. Your future is too bright to hide in your father's shadow. What will *your* next step look like? What are *you* willing to do?" Sophia asks, hoping to reach Claire's soul.

Just then, Sophia witnesses a flickering spark, brighten from the depths of Claire's heart. She remembers Naseem's guidance, to 'connect with Claire des Tenebres'. Approaching her, till they are face to face, Sophia asks, "Your name, Claire des Tenebres, it means, 'Light out of Darkness', correct?"

"Yes..." Claire responds, but she is distracted, looking into her hand at the stone.

"Then live up to it!" Sophia challenges her one last time, just as the guards bring forth the leader of the chanting voices, releasing him, steps away from Claire's moment of truth. He stands before her, hands lifted toward Claire as if to welcome the courageous spirit he sees within her.

Claire's intuition begins to inform her as the connection with the love surrounding her grows stronger. The Light energy has found its way to her heart and is awaiting her next move. As Claire begins to feel the power of this Light, she walks closer to the elder. She grasps his uplifted hands and declares, "It's *my* time! Success is defined in many ways, and I choose to find another."

Claire looks deep into the Chief's eyes when she states, "Together, we will succeed as one." Her intentions spill out with her warm tears. "We will work together, to find harmony for this land and your people. This is a promise I am now ready to keep."

"Then it is so!" he exclaims through his wonderful, toothless smile. Their spirits bond in this special moment. Claire finds the courage to step out of her father's shadow. It is clear, Light is guiding her thoughts, words and actions...as she follows the wisdom heard deep within, "Seek Truth and you will find your potential!"

Claire walks over and places the stone into Sophia's palm, "Thank you, for breaking through my walls and showing me the power within. I hope that we will have the chance to meet again."

Sophia senses a mystic embrace from Rose, before reluctantly, but honestly saying, "The stone has found its home for now. Here it shall remain as a reminder of your promise to stay connected to the Light. One day, I hope very soon, it will find its way back to a sanctuary for peace in a haven of hope." Sophia begins to envision a beautiful time. "When you are ready, you will share your memories of the ideals that are now forming as your future plans. Until we meet again, the stone is yours." She leaves them with that vision, to race for the Anastasia, which is soon to depart for home.

CHAPTER TWENTY-FIVE

As Sophia departs the lobby of ∞ Infinity Mining Company, she wraps her long veil around her shoulders for solace, accepting that the stone is no longer in her possession. There is no time left for second thoughts, it's late, very late. She must run to reach the Anastasia before 6:00PM. She rounds the corner in full stride as she sees the mighty ship loaded with cargo and passengers. The crew is beginning to release the massive ropes that keep her restrained. Sophia hears a loud, "Last call...ALL ABOARD!!" as the gangway is being untethered from the dock.

"There is no way I'm missing the boat home." With three giant strides she leaps upon the gangway, her mystic veil giving her the extra lift she needs to climb aboard. The horn blasts. Anastasia is leaving her berth and venturing toward the open seas.

From the starboard side of the ship, Sophia can see Beatrix; all but a few of her lights have now dimmed. Just as the Captain described, there were hundreds of scavengers on board, bidding for her wares. At the back of the ship, balancing upon Beatrix' metal railing, she sees the Captain. He is lowering her flag. It will be the one memento of his graceful ship that he will keep. The Captain looks up, as if Sophia's light is guiding him through this last port of call. He salutes to her in gratitude then slowly departs his ship one final time as the wind whispers the truth into the night, "The vessel dies but the Spirit lives on."

CHAPTER TWENTY-SIX

Anastasia has been skimming the calm seas for the past several days, but this last night of sailing has turned into quite a battle. The seas are surging with menacing waves cresting high around the sides of the ship. Each wave is fighting to leave its watery home, like a rebellious youth seeking to establish his individuality, only to fall back into the mysterious depths once again.

All the passengers, including Sophia, hunker down in their cabins for the duration of the storm. As night falls, so does she, into a bumpy night of restless sleep. Images, dreams and visions are imprisoned by a nightmare of the distant divide she foresees. Rain is beating down hard against the ship as she slowly makes her way toward her last port. The smell of Anastasia's exertion is wafting up from the engine room, filling the cabins with the smell of burning oil. Sophia's physical senses begin to submerge into the nightmare...

In the wee hours of the night, Anastasia approaches the far off land with engines slowed to a quiet hum. The darkened skies attempt to shield her from an unnerving sight. In the distance, a sacred land is pummeled with rockets as heavy black smoke rises above it. Loud explosions set an unsteady rhythm, sending percussion waves out in every direction. The wind carries the smell of burning tires and rotting garbage-- the repulsive scents of war--toward the ship as a warning to stay clear of this place. Fear has found a home in this land, and built a giant wall to imprison each soul.

The turmoil beleaguers Sophia until she gets out of bed. She watches from the ship's window for a view into the darkness, but the rain won't let the images through. The drops keep pouring down as if the heavens are attempting to cleanse the land of the evil that hatred breeds. Yet, off in the distance, the boom, boom, boom of exploding mortar shells persist.

As the ship pushes ever closer to the war-torn land; Sophia senses the fear rising from both sides of the massive wall. She rushes out of her cabin door, past the crew, and up onto the deck so she can witness the battles being waged: separation of man from woman, black from white, faith from Truth! The walls of separation are many and varied, but they only protect fear.

Once she reaches the edge of the ship's railing she is aghast at the scene. Along the dividing wall, men, women and children are all blindly screaming at the *other* side. Rocks and rockets are being thrown. The tortures committed upon this land produce streams of blood from the hilltops to the edges of the ocean. Blood stains the sand, as tears stain the cheeks of innocent children.

As Sophia witnesses the battle lines being drawn, a gust of wind screams the truth, "Separation is the first cause of inequality!" Each side forces their fight, their faith, and their will upon the other. Each is prepared to fight to the death...even that of his brothers'. The chaos builds as Sophia watches helplessly from her perch on the ship.

She begins to feel the jagged vibrations of hateful energy rising from the land. She is close enough to understand the history behind the sharp-edged emotion. This fear has been years in the making. It masquerades as a *just cause* while devouring all forms of freedom and dignity. The peoples' voices begin to rise, without any expectation of being heard. Soon enough, they are cut down and silenced. The evil is overwhelming as it begins to spread across the borders and traverses the sea. Sophia can feel the fear move in closer; she can feel it surrounding her.

She calls upon her inner light to expel this fear from the land and to unite its people with love. But the forces behind the wall are many and far reaching. Repeatedly she calls upon her inner light for guidance, but the darkness surrounding her prevails.

Sophia races back to her cabin to retrieve her veil. "Surely, with my sacred veil I can bring love and compassion to these people." She grabs the veil and runs out on deck. While facing the divided land, she stands on top of the highest rung of the ship's railing, arms lifted high, with her veil above her, fighting against the winds of war. She is being blown from side to side by the violent gusts that are fleeing the land with each explosion. Repeatedly she beckons, "Bring peace upon the land and within the hearts of its leaders!" But still the darkness prevails. Sophia digs deeper and deeper to summon her power of light just as one massive blast steals her from the ship and carries her to the ocean floor.

She struggles violently to swim to the top, but the evil energy drags her down to the darkest pit of the ocean. It pins her there and threatens to extinguish the Light for all time. With this force her body goes limp, and her fingers loosen their faithful grip upon her sacred veil. It too, falls to the ocean floor, lying next to Sophia's lifeless body.

Sophia feels her spirit gently lifting away from her body. Up, up, up she is flying with greater speed until her body is out of site, left behind in the murky waters. She soars out of the ocean and into the cosmos, swirling and twirling higher at infinite speed. The wonder of the cosmic lift inspires awe within her soul. Upon seeing the full glory of the cosmos she declares, "This must be heaven! Oh, the stars are spectacular. They are dancing orbs of light." The cosmos embraces her as she soars, higher and higher.

Sophia begins to take in every atom of this precious view. "This sweet smell of paradise—it is the scent of cookies crisping in the oven. This truly feels like I have come home." She quiets her thoughts as she hears distant echoes resonating from the stars. They are the tones of bells and hums that could only be made by angels. The sounds begin to flow through her as her spirit enlivens with the energy of the angels. They are embracing her with a fullness of Love that brings her to the pinnacle of perfect contentment. Sophia feels at peace while being cradled by this loving energy.

Then the bliss of the moment is broken by the thoughts the angels manifest through Sophia. Their message is solemn but full of truth. "My dear Sophia, your work has not been completed. It is not your time. You must return, to reach your full potential." With those words Sophia is gently guided back down toward Earth. Her spirit departs from the beauty of this starry home and submerges into the ocean waters once again.

With an electrifying jolt, she is reunited with the unmoving corpse that lies on the ocean floor. Instantly, Sophia's heart pulsates back to life. The stirring about agitates the currents around Sophia, lifting her sacred veil into sight. She grabs the veil just as another ocean current lifts her above the surface of the water and throws her back onto the deck of the ship.

The impact forces a gush of ocean swill from her lungs as she gasps between coughs for a breath of fresh air. She is exhausted and the bitter taste of frustration still persists as she is sprawled out upon the deck. Slowly her strength builds along with her resolve. She yells out to the evil that challenges her so, "My Light will never be dimmed by fear!"

Sophia defiantly tries again to bring peace across the land, but she repeatedly fails.

She asks the heavens, "Why can't I help them? Am I doing everything within my power? What is wrong with me!?" The answers don't come. She leans back against the ship's cabin, hugging her knees like a lost child, and rocking herself back and forth for comfort. She begins to mourn her failure. "I have let these souls down." She weeps as she sees each person's fear being imprinted upon their future actions, reinforcing the hatred that imprisons their souls and perpetuates every act of evil. They blindly fault each other for the darkness that surrounds them, as fear continues to play with their minds. "Why can't they see, they each have the power to awaken the Light within?"

Her ego is attempting to rule over her spirit. She can feel her crafty ego manipulating her frustration into anger as she calls out one more time, "Help me! Give me the strength to bring peace on this earth!" With tremendous fury, her fist slams down onto the sacred veil that lies crumpled by her side. The powerful energy she calls forth shoots out into the Universe from the four corners of the mystic cloth. The response rebounds back instantly.

Hovering all around Sophia are the images of her four Sages: Astar, Rose, Ama and Naseem. No one is pleased by the manner in which they have been summoned. They surround her immediately to calm the waves of harsh energy she is sending out to the Universe. One by one they begin to soothe the energy and guide Sophia to her true intentions. Naseem calms the severity of the winds around them. Ama softens the heavy rains and brings about beauty and gentleness. Rose encircles all with loving kindness, as Astar begins imparting a little wisdom about Sophia's demands upon her inner light.

Astar softly delves into Sophia's thoughts, "My darling Sophia, what is it that you're trying to accomplish? State your intentions clearly so we can all understand."

"Oh Astar, I've heard the desperate voices calling out to me in fear of the hatred that feeds upon this land. I want to tear down the walls that fear builds. If I could just lower these walls, and raise their consciousness…will people unite? Will they choose Love over fear?" When Sophia hears her own spoken words, she realizes something is futile in her efforts. But, without the guidance of her Sages, she cannot connect with the Wisdom that is within her.

The Elders are all too familiar with Sophia's impassioned calling upon humanity. They can feel the fire that fuels her wishes for a united land and common ground within the minds of all. They too dream of a time when all of humanity will be living in peace amongst the cosmos.

Astar lovingly embraces Sophia as she explains, "My dear Sophia, you cannot awaken the Light in anyone but yourself. All you can do is be a beacon of this Light and reveal its Splendor. Some will see the path to take, and others are not *yet* ready to take these steps. It is when the Light shines brightly within all of humanity that you will see your desires come true. It is inevitable. People will, one day, choose to connect with their inner Light. They will choose Love, but we cannot foresee when this day will come. All we can do is to be the bearers of this Light, and patiently await the awakening."

Rose embraces Sophia with loving kindness once again as she begins, "Sophia, you are not alone in this magnificent desire. The Universe itself is awaiting the enlightenment of all its inhabitants. Stay connected to the Spirit of Love, and light the path for others, in hopes that they too will soon find the Spirit within themselves."

The four sages encircle Sophia with the clear light of Love then softly fade away, leaving Sophia amidst their wise words. She is quietly still, pondering her visions and wondering if she will ever encounter the people of this nation again. For now, her nightmares continue, but she is left with the peace of knowing that free will finds the Light within each one of us, in due time.

CHAPTER TWENTY-SEVEN

The light of the sun beaming into the cabin awakens Sophia. She moves slowly atop the sweat-soaked covers of the bed. The battle scenes of her vivid nightmare left her tired and beaten. Her loyal veil is still tightly held within her palm. It too appears a little worse for wear from the passage of last night.

The calls of the crew, securing the ship and tightening her ropes, echo in the small but busy harbor in Palamo Port. Anastasia completes her silent promise to cross the vast ocean and safely deliver her passengers to their loved ones.

Sophia hurries to clean herself up and get ready to disembark. It won't be long now, before she can wrap her arms around her father and receive the hugs she missed so dearly over the past seven years.

The people at the dock are getting louder as they crowd the ship, eagerly awaiting the release of her passengers.

After a speedy shower and some quick packing, Sophia is ready. She runs down to the deck to view the scene below. To her great surprise there is a huge crowd of townspeople with signs and banners, all welcoming her home. In front of the friendly crowd stands her father who is full of anticipation, her guiding star—Astar, who foresaw her arrival and the old tribal leader, who is eager to welcome this rainbow of light named Sophia.

Time seems to move ever so slowly as she watches the crew complete their tasks. The ship's ropes are dripping with salt water and seaweed as they hold Anastasia steady while the crew releases the gangway.

Sophia stands atop the passageway to her father's loving embrace, as she sees him in the bustling crowd. Once their eyes meet, it is as if she is a child once again. Joyful tears roll down both their smiling faces just as the ropes allow the passengers to go ashore.

Roger runs to hug his beloved daughter. He holds her tightly, as if he will never again let her go. Both their hearts join in celebration as the throng of friends and villagers swarm them up and begin exchanging hugs and words of welcome.

Soon, they all make their way from the port toward Hope's Haven. There is an unbroken line of visitors driving up the road to the entrance of the grounds. As Sophia approaches the archway leading home; her past images of the peaceful sanctuary blossom into reality. Just as she envisioned, the home nestles softly into its surroundings, blending quietly with the gentle energy of Nature herself.

At the entrance to the forty-acre parcel there stands the beautiful metal archway. Entwined, in flowering ivy, between the wrought-iron are the words, 'Hope's Haven, A Sanctuary for Peace'. Sophia gets out of the vehicle, into the brilliance of the land. She is bursting with excitement to see more as she runs ahead of the crowd to the luscious meadows and then to the gardens surrounding the house. She visually takes in the beautiful grounds while breathing in the rich scent of the moist earth beneath her feet. Her senses fill with memories of the past wonders she has uncovered upon this land. Sophia runs further to the garden gate in front the mansion. She walks through the gate and stops at a graceful weeping willow to take in its elegant beauty. She gently runs her hands along each flowing strand of leaves, as the breeze welcomes her home with a kiss on the forehead.

The others pull up the long gravel drive as the party begins and grows into a celebration. The townspeople join together in passing along a steady stream of warm sentiments. Everyone is welcome! The local tribe performs throughout the afternoon with poetry, music and dances as they give thanks to the rainbow light that now lives amongst them. The celebration continues until the tip of dusk, when the last guests retire to their village homes. Sophia and her father stand at the gate, waving good-bye as the evening mist rolls in, concealing the star-filled skies.

Astar approaches the two with an oil lamp, as dusk makes itself comfortable atop Hope's Haven. "Sophia dear, I want to make sure you can see the steps in front of you my dear. Take this time to reconnect with your father. Goodnight all. I'll see you at first light." Astar leaves the two of them, with the light of the lamp, at the garden gate.

"Goodnight Astar, thank you for all that you've done." Roger calls out.

Then, Sophia sends the telepathic message, "…and all that you do."

Astar heads inside to allow the reunion of father and daughter much needed private time. "You're both welcome."

she calls out over her shoulder, smiling at the two as she walks toward the door. She stops, looks back at Sophia and winks, then turns in for the night.

Sophia lifts the lamp to light their pathway from the garden gate to the entrance of the home. That's when she notices the round stepping stones, the same ones her father had been etching so diligently in her vision. Each stone has an incredible symbol crafted upon it. Each symbol rests in its rightful place, along the path. "Dad...these symbols...how do you know about them?" Sophia kneels down to the first hand-carved disk. "They are beautiful and perfect in every detail." She traces her fingers around the circle which appears to be balancing atop the letter 'T'. "These are the sacred symbols, the ones that mark the path to my Sages' cottage." Now, here they are, marking the pathway to the heart of her home:

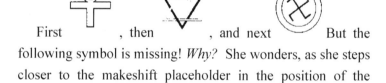

First   , then   , and next   But the following symbol is missing! *Why?* She wonders, as she steps closer to the makeshift placeholder in the position of the fourth symbol   , the mystic circle.

Her curious mind begins, "Dad, how did you capture these symbols in perfect detail? And do you know that there's one missing?" She asks while admiring her father's impeccable accuracy upon each stone.

Roger scratches his head then with a tone of frustration, he explains, "Ah, that one. It's been eluding me. It is the most frustrating thing. You know, I have been able to design and build this entire house, yet I can't carve this one circular symbol by hand. Every time I try to bring it to life, I am not able to get the two ends to meet. This one's a tough one, alright."

With those words Sophia revisits the nightmare of her own frustration. This symbol of unity eludes her as well.

Her curiosity calls her attention back to the stones and her father's knowledge of the symbols as she asks, "But how do you know about every detail, how do you know about these symbols at all?"

Roger explains, "The images methodically entered my thoughts. I would sit right over there, on that rocking chair and anticipate your journey home. Then images, of the path from a mystic mountain-top home back to Hope's Haven, would fill my thoughts. Along the way, I was compelled to create each of these symbols; in this intricate detail, no less. The impulses were strong and persistent, and the imagery was crystal clear. It was a blessing too, because etching these stones helped me 'chip away the time', until you came home to me." Roger amuses himself with his own pun.

Sophia glances over each step as she begins to make the connection. Along her journey, whenever she witnessed the awakening of Light in those around her, her father must have perceived the corresponding symbol as well. Just as Sophia observed the symbols manifest above the inn keeper, the Captain and Claire, the symbols would then appear within her father's connected consciousness.

Sophia stands on the placeholder for the one symbol that eludes them both. As she rocks herself back and forth on the loose disk, she hears the voices of her Sages once again, "All in due time. There is still inner work to be done, by all. Until then, the Universe awaits our awakening." The surrounding mist begins to give way, as the moon reflects the Wisdom of the symbols.

After lingering in the serenity of the gardens well into the night, Roger and Sophia enter their home. Standing in the grand foyer, Sophia takes her sacred veil from the table, as Roger helps her up the magnificent staircase. He shows her to the room he created for his daughter. Due to all the celebrations of the afternoon, this is her first look through the beautiful mansion.

At the top of the stairs, they walk into the right wing of the upper floor. She smiles at the familiarity of the layout. Amazingly, the room resembles Rose's cottage, only bigger. The impressively large room is warm and surprisingly cozy with a fireplace and an alcove in the center of the wall. Her father built a huge wrap-around deck, where she can recline back and drift amongst the stars each night. Sophia is grateful for the thoughtfulness of every detail within this home.

She approaches a feature that she first saw at Rose's cottage, where her view of the area was only from in front of Rose's mystic veil. She honored Rose so much that she never thought of peeking behind it; not even once! Here, she sees three steps that lead to a raised landing. "Dad, what's this little room for?" She pokes her head into the mysterious landing as Roger walks up from behind her and ventures up the few steps.

He begins, "I made a quiet spot for you to be alone with your thoughts. You can gather your personal library of reading materials right here on these shelves." He pushes on one very special bookshelf as it spins open to reveal a winding staircase. "Whenever you get that urge to explore the meadows in the wee hours of the night, you can run down your private stairwell into the rose garden and beyond."

Her father continues to encourage Sophia's connection with Nature. She is deeply moved by this secret access to her quiet place of discovery. "I love it Dad. It's all so perfect!"

She then looks back at the opening to this quiet landing and declares, "This will be the spot to hang my veil—my treasured gift from Rose." She spreads the sacred veil across the small walkway atop the steps. As she holds the midnight-blue fabric, she reminisces with the images of Rose bursting from behind her mystic veil each morning.

The moonlight shimmers upon the veil, drawing Sophia's attention to the bands of growth once again. The question remains, "How could this veil have grown?"

Then her intuition begins informing her. She sees three distinct bands of growth. As her hand graces each one, the voices of gratitude are heard over the winds of the Universe. The inn keeper, the Captain and the CEO each express their appreciation through the vibrations of the mystic veil.

Sophia wraps herself into the beautiful energy of the veil as she turns to look around her new room with tremendous appreciation for her father's creation. "Everything is picture-perfect, Dad. You have made this a wonderful home in which Love will grow."

CHAPTER TWENTY-EIGHT

Sophia walks around the mansion grounds to a natural spring within the meadow. She sits beside the water to watch the ripples give way to tranquility in the far reaches of the pond. The woodland creatures sense the brilliance of love shining upon their meadow once again. They slowly come out of the woods to greet Sophia and be in her company. It is as if she never parted from them at all. As they surround her, one by one, she receives warm nuzzles from bunnies, and cold wet noses brushing up under her hand, as a doe and her young fawn move in closer to Sophia's love. All of Nature welcomes her home as the birds announce her return to the meadow.

It's only been eight weeks since her arrival back home. She spends most of her time in the gardens and meadows, pondering the potential for Hope's Haven and the Sanctuary for Peace it promises to become.

Her thoughts drift away to the souls she has met along her journey. The image of the inn keeper and his wife flashes into her thoughts as she hears the wise words of her Sages, "Stay connected to the Spirit of Love, and light the path for others."

A loud creak from the garden gate announces the arrival of a visitor. Sophia runs around to the front garden, where her eyes meet with an inspired seeker of Truth. A hearty-sized man with one small sack of clothes is standing just inside the gate.

Sophia smiles up to the skies, toward the mystic presence of her Sages, as she notices this man is atop the first stepping stone within the Sanctuary of Peace. This step holds the symbol of the Tree of Life—the knowledge of good and evil. Standing right on top of the symbol, as if to claim it as his new found path in life, is the inn keeper himself.

By her light, he has found his path. Upon this path he seeks to reach his full potential. Sophia's bright aura guides him to seek a life worth living.

Upon seeing Sophia once again, he begins to tear up. He is filled with gratitude, joy and trust. He chokes back his tears as he stammers, "Um, ma'am, yer note said 'seek truth'…and my wife…well…she said yu'd be here so…um, so I left everythin' I knew to find ya…and…well, I found dis place. Maybe, I cud stay a while?"

Sophia runs to him with a joyful heart. She softly takes his arm and leads him up the steps of the Sanctuary for Peace, where she asks, for the first time, "What is your name? After all that we've been through, I don't even know your name."

"Earnest, ma'am…My name is Earnest."

"Well Earnest…" she opens the door, and confesses with a warm smile, "…we've been waiting for you; we thought you would never get here." She giggles while thinking of Rose's warm greeting to her upon entering the Sages' cottage for the first time.

Astar peeks out from the kitchen window as she knowingly calls out, "I'll put the kettle on. We have our first seeker!"

Over the next several weeks and months, the Sanctuary for Peace welcomes many seekers. Some come to find the path to Peace, some just to be in the presence of it, but all come with the spark of Love in their hearts.

Earnest continues to gain wisdom and to strengthen his inner light. He learns from everyone and everything within his new environment. Each day, he looks forward to Astar's gift of storytelling. She always leaves him with a nugget of love, and a lesson for life, woven between each tale. Their time together improves Earnests' mastery of the English language. For this too, he is grateful, since his street-wise speech always left him feeling as if he is undeserving of a peaceful life.

Earnest spends many days hiking deep within the woods surrounding the Sanctuary where Nature shares her wisdom with him. His daily hikes reshape his thoughts and his physique as he builds both his body and mind with the same balance found in Nature.

He especially honors the time he spends with Roger, as stories filled with Hope teach him of how to truly love with depth and gentleness. Earnest and Roger build a relationship based upon trust. Roger becomes a magnificent father-figure. One filled with caring, discipline, love and trust; all the characteristics that eluded the relationship between Earnest and his own father during his painful childhood.

One day, Earnest leans on their bond of trust as he asks, "Roger, can I ask you something? It's kind of personal."

Roger is patiently carving a piece of oak as he responds, "Sure thing Earnest, you can ask me anything. You know that."

"Well, Roger, um...how come you never re-married? Aren't you lonely?" Earnest's questions hang in the stillness for a long time before Roger responds.

Roger puts the carving knife down. He leans back in his chair in silence for another moment, then he says, "You know Earnest...the ancients seem to believe that each one of us has another half within this Universe. These two halves are in communication with each other, across the cosmos; waiting to unite over time. When we meet and unite, we uplift each other's soul to a higher realm.

"When I met my wife Hope, I found my soul-mate, I found my other half. There is no other, not for me." He starts carving again. "...and as for being lonely...I know that Hope is with me, always. Whenever I need her, I just go to her realm in my thoughts, and there she is."

Roger's words deeply move Earnest. He imagines his own wife back home at the Inn. Up until this point, he couldn't bear the thought of letting go of her completely. He repeatedly avoided signing the divorce documents. But now, he understands why there could never be bliss between the two of them. Their connection is based on desire, passion and lust. He lusts for her physical beauty, and she desires his ill-gotten gain, at any cost. Earnest now understands that when the fire of lust burns out, all one is left with is ashes. It is only through the Light of Love, that he will reach his potential.

That same afternoon, upon returning to his room, Earnest signs and mails the documents, releasing his final hold on his past. He writes his wife to let her know that the Inn and any of his belongings are hers to keep, along with her freedom. He wishes for her, the peace that he is finding within himself.

Earnest looks out his bedroom window and sees Sophia in the gardens. She continues to walk within the Light, as an example of the power of Love that he finds within himself. She exudes the wisdom of Nature, of Light and of Love in her daily life. Her aura continues to strengthen. She is a rainbow of light that brilliantly reflects the Spirit of Love in all that she does.

Slowly the mansion is becoming a gathering place for a growing number of seekers, townspeople and new comers alike. With each new visitor the path from fear toward Love brightens and becomes clear. Each soul is finding or strengthening its connection to the Light. As the seekers of truth grow in number, so does the power of their united energy. It is said that the light, from two candles, shines farther when they are united, this light shines brightly upon Hope's Haven, awaiting others to unite with their inner Light.

CHAPTER TWENTY-NINE

Roger and Sophia cherish the daily walks to Hope's oak tree. Roger carefully preserved the space during all the construction that took place on this sacred hill. The bench, the stone fire pit and the trinity of symbols, including the beautiful infinity that Sophia made so many years ago, complete the scene for their daily exchange of stories and memories.

Each morning, the ocean mist surrounds the grounds, engulfing the valley below. Up on the hill, the mansion and this beautiful oak tree pierce through the delicate mist, allowing sunlight to bless this land. Sophia calls the morning mist, the hug of angel's wings as the feathery clouds encircle their hill.

Roger senses the presence of Hope as the wind whispers the words "I will be with you always," forever warming his heart. He feels the breeze place a gentle kiss on the back of his neck as he remembers his dear wife.

The past two years, since Sophia's return, have flown by so quickly. Everyone is quite busy within the Peace Sanctuary, as they continue to welcome the curious and the serious seekers alike. All are welcome. The home is glowing with the inquisitive energy of those who visit, and the Universe welcomes their open-hearted explorations.

It takes plenty of work to keep up with the growing daily routines, but it is truly a labor of Love.

This morning, Astar is preparing to go into town with her shopping list, when Sophia offers to go instead. Something is tugging at Sophia's intuition and she knows to listen carefully to it.

"Astar, would you mind if I went into town for you today? It will give me a chance to see what's new in the shop windows. I feel like there's something there for me to find." Sophia predicts, as she runs up the stairs to change her clothes.

Astar wraps an apron around herself and calls up the staircase, "I would love it, my dear. That will give me time to start on lunch. It will be ready for you when you return." She senses the electricity in the air too. She feels something energizing their surroundings as she patiently waits to see what the future unfolds.

Sophia sits on the bed to put on her shoes; she notices an image upon her sacred veil. A very young boy is sitting alone at a wishing well, praying. She approaches the shimmering veil, but the reflection is faint. She senses the urgency to leave now as her intuition pulls her toward town.

She runs down the stairs, grabs Astar's list and rushes out the door. Sophia reaches the village in no time as she turns the corner onto Main Street, heading toward the port. She listens again for clues from her intuition, but all she hears is the clip-clop sound of her shoes upon the old wooden planks of the raised sidewalks. She slowly meanders through town and peers into the big picture windows; each one displays the newest wares in the store-fronts of this quaint port town.

Sophia is stumped at why she feels the urgency to be present in this time and space. The tugging at her intuition has subsided as she slows her pace and looks around for a sign of some sort.

When nothing turns up, she retrieves Astar's shopping list and proceeds to the General Store. She stops at the doorway to read the list, when her intuition heightens again. She is drawn to a very young boy, not more than five years old, who is inside the shop. He is squatting in front of the candy aisle, looking longingly at the sweet delights. He slowly turns his head to peek over his shoulder at the doorway where Sophia is standing. He turns back and gingerly places the candy bar in his hand back onto the shelf.

She is intrigued with the young boy's slow and deliberate action. As she enters through the doorway her intuition whispers, "His hunger is concealing, this desperate act of stealing."

The young boy watches Sophia enter the store. He stands and looks up at her with tear-filled eyes. He then reaches into the pocket of his torn pants and hesitantly puts another bar of chocolate back in its rightful place on the shelf.

Touched by his tears, Sophia approaches him with a caring smile, "Well hello young man." She picks up the two bars of chocolate and pays for them. Then she walks outside, plunks herself down on the wooden sidewalk, and waits.

Ever so slowly the young boy walks out of the store, all the while looking at Sophia with a silent sense of wonder. He is fascinated by her, yet apprehensive of her in the same instance.

"Would you like to join me? I don't think I could finish both chocolate bars all by myself. Come here. Tell me, what's your name?" Sophia pats the wooden planks next to her, motioning him to take a seat. When he does so, she offers him a bar of sweetness.

He can't stop looking at her in awe, even though his hunger is coaxing him to grab the chocolate. "My name is Cody." He answers while timidly reaching for the candy. Upon their hands connecting, the images of Cody's childhood flood into Sophia's visions.

As the thoughts fill her mind, she sees the truth. This boy is not a thief, he is an orphan. Five years ago when he was a baby, the man who had fathered him, during one lost night of passion, was called back to his military post. His father died violently while in a war-torn land, far away. His unwed mother turned to drugs in order to soften the pains of her loneliness. The addiction stole Cody's mother away from him too, just a few weeks ago. He has been alone in the streets, trying to survive, ever since.

Sophia places her arm around the boy's shoulders and tells him, "You don't have to be alone any longer. We will find the path to a love-filled home. I know just where to start."

He looks up at Sophia, as he innocently asks her, "Why wasn't I enough? Why did my mom leave me too? Why was I ever born if no one wants me?" Tears flow down his cheeks....and then down Sophia's, as she senses his little, broken heart.

Sophia feels a rush of breeze wrap around them; her own mother's angelic words fill her heart as she comforts the young boy. Lifting his sweet face, she looks him in the eyes and says, "Why were you born? Well Cody…God created you, to see what you would show Him."

With those words he moves in closer to Sophia, until he is tucked in tightly under her care. He wipes his wet nose into his shirt sleeve and confesses, "When I saw you at the door, I thought you were my mom for a second, but then I saw the rainbow around you, and I knew you were an angel. I'm right, aren't I? The last thing Mommy told me was that angels would watch over me. You're my angel, the one I've been praying for at the wishing well!"

Sophia is at a loss for words as this boy's story fills her heart. She doesn't know what the future holds for them, but she knows she can't leave him alone to roam the streets another moment. They spend the rest of the morning close together, like two peas in a pod. Sophia finishes up her errands in town with her young helper close at hand. The two slowly become inseparable as the bond of trust grows with each step they take along the way home.

Back at home, Astar is in the kitchen cooking up lunch and it smells delicious. The savory goodness wafts out onto the porch and teases Roger's appetite. He enters the kitchen eager to taste the yummy concoction.

"Astar that smells so good, I've got to do a taste test…its mandatory." He chuckles as he reaches for a spoon to dip into the aromatic pot. "Mmmmm, that is wonderful! I wish I knew what you do to food to make it taste so heavenly."

As he goes in for another "taste", Astar gives the back of his hand a quick smack as she giggles, "Use a clean spoon, young man…no double-dipping." She loves it when people enjoy her tasty meals. A warm pot of goodness is a great way of bringing people together.

Just then a vision comes to Astar, a young boy double-timing his little footsteps to keep up with Sophia. The two of them are filled with excitement and chatter as they quickly walk across the driveway. His tear-stained cheeks are now stretched to a wide and happy smile.

Astar feels the electricity in the air again as she joyfully requests, "Roger would you please place another setting for lunch? We're having company."

Roger turns to ask Astar about this mystery guest, just as Sophia and young Cody come up the garden path. Cody is amazed at the sight. He is stepping and tripping over himself while taking in all the glorious sights around Hope's Haven. He looks at the mansion in bewilderment and asks, "Angel Sophia, is this where you live? Is this heaven?"

Sophia is warmed by his innocence and curiosity. "Cody, this is our home, we're in Hope's Haven. Come on in, I want you to meet my family and friends. I know they will love to get to know you." The smell of Astar's good old home cooking excites them both as they enter the home.

Astar comes from the kitchen with a big-hearted hug for young Cody, as if she has known him for years. It has been so long since he felt a soft motherly-hug filled with love. Cody melts into Astar's kindness. Her love banishes any remaining fears that crept into his lonesome thoughts. His one wish is that his days of wandering alone in the streets and nights of hiding in darkened doorways, come to an end. He imagines himself staying here in Hope's Haven, right in the big loving embrace of Astar's tight hug.

Her warm voice charms him, "Who is this young man we have here? He is the best hugger I've ever met, I know that for sure! Are you hungry son? C'mon with me, let's get something tasty into your belly then we can share some stories."

Cody takes Sophia's hand and looks up at Astar and offers his hand to her as well. He feels the love surrounding him and he welcomes it. "My name is Cody. Are you an angel *too*?"

Astar smiles and gives Cody a playful wink. She then softly whispers into his ear, "That's our little secret, yours and mine."

Sophia adores how Astar works her sweet magic. Cody is falling under the spell of Love, just like Sophia had done when she first received Astar's warm embrace. No one can resist feeling loved in her presence.

Astar calls out to everyone, "Lunch is ready, come and get it!" as they all enter the kitchen. Sophia helps Cody wash up and find a seat around the table, while Roger gives Astar a hand with serving this delicious meal.

Earnest runs into the kitchen, breathless from his morning hike. "Astar, I ran the last half-mile, led by the smell of your home-cooking!" He washes his hands then walks behind Cody without noticing the little guy. He then sits right across the table from him. Earnest doesn't see the curly blonde hair and big blue eyes that are peeking up from the edge of the table.

When Earnest finally lifts his gaze to greet everyone he is taken aback by the little boy. Earnest sinks back into his chair and looks around with a highly inquisitive expression upon his befuddled face. First he looks at Astar, then at the little boy....then he quickly tries to gain Roger's attention as he looks back at the little boy...finally he locks eyes with Sophia as he nods his head toward Cody as if to let her know 'there is a stranger amongst us'.

Sophia keeps her giggles contained while Earnest keeps his eyes locked on Sophia, almost afraid to look at Cody again. "Earnest, I'd like you to meet Cody. He will be staying with us for a while." Earnest is so surprised by this young visitor; he is acting as if he has never been around a child before. The truth is, he hasn't, really. Sophia tries to break the silence, "Earnest! Don't you want to say hello?"

Cody stands up and reaches his tiny hand across the table to grab a hold of Earnest's huge palm for a strong 'manly' shake. "Hello Er-nist. Hey, your hand is really big...it feels like a baseball mitt!" Cody announces without any inhibitions.

That one line melts the ice! Earnest begins shaking Cody's hand in return and laughing, "Well, hello Cody...maybe after lunch we can go outside and catch some balls with this big ol' mitt."

Sophia's vision catches a glimpse of the future. The Universe seems to bring each of us exactly what is needed to have Love grow.

CHAPTER THIRTY

The news, of a sanctuary tucked in the hills of Palamo Port, makes its way across land and sea. Over the past few years Hope's Haven welcomes visitors from many nations. An entire room adjacent to the library is dedicated to the cards and notes from the seekers of the past. The notes express gratitude in a multitude of languages. Each note brings back the electric energy of the souls that chart their path by the guiding Light within.

The message, "Seek Truth, and you will find your potential" is retold in many varied and beautiful ways along these walls. The stories of mended relationships, new found careers, selfless acts of philanthropy, and even spontaneous healings are repeated countlessly as if they were stars in the heavenly skies. Each story is uniquely beautiful; each story contributes to the splendor of life.

Today's mail delivery has a bounty of cards and letters, but one envelope catches Sophia's attention. Just a corner of the envelope is peeking out from under the pile, it is just enough for Sophia to make out her precious symbol, ∞.

She retrieves the envelope from amongst the rest, and runs her fingers along the symbol. Joy fills her heart as the essence of the letter enlightens her thoughts. She rips the envelope open to read each detail aloud:

Dear Sophia,

A promise reveals its value once it is kept...

It has been a few years since we last met. You stood in my grand office as you witnessed my promise to Chief Rongomau. On that day, in your light, I gave my word to him and his people to protect their ancestral land. My words quickly turned into actions as if angels created the blueprints for my future.

A plan for building upon this site came together within weeks of my decision to stop all mining efforts. I met a great architect and a beautiful landscape designer whom I appointed as my partners for this project. They helped to bring my promise to life. They have been gifts from heaven, not only for me, but also for Chief Rongomau and for all the people of this land. One day soon, I would love for you to meet my partners, Naseem and Ama, for none of this would have been possible without their support.

Sophia stops reading to look up at Astar in astonishment, "Can it be true? Did Naseem and Ama have a hand in this Astar?"

Astar confesses with her warm signature smile, "Of course they did, and I'm sure Rose had a few points of input too, my dear. You didn't expect Claire to do everything alone, did you? Oh no ma'am, we never go it alone...the Universe sends us guidance the moment we express our Spirit-filled will."

Sophia shakes her head with adoration for her sages as she continues reading Claire's letter.

Together we constructed a humble yet prosperous site, where visitors can learn, work, and live with the native people of this land. You should see the guest cottages we built for those who wish to stay with us to learn more about the peaceful ways of these indigenous people.

We have named the site in honor of Chief Rongomau. It is called The Rongo Center for Universal Harmony...Rongo for short.

We also built an Oceanic Institute with an educational program for young seafarers from all around the world, teaching them sustainable ways to honor the seas and keep them blue. Our resident instructor is an amazing old Sea Captain who wandered into the building just before its completion. He said he had been seeking a resurrection of sorts, as he was forced to retire his ship and his job at the same time. Once inside the building he proclaimed a "calling" to continue his work here, at the Oceanic Institute, and he has been with us ever since. The Captain shares a great many lessons of crossing the oceans and the mysteries held within the deep waters. His presence enlivens the spirit of all of our students and visitors.

Sophia I must admit though, not everything was a smooth transition. I was discharged of all my duties as CEO of the Infinity Mining Company. My father and his board of directors made sure of it once they audited the return on their investment at our new site.

Between you and me, I think they are using the wrong unit of measure; they spend far too much energy counting their coins instead of their blessings.

I have left the darkness of my past within the confines of that boardroom. I asked for and was given the deed to this plat of land as my severance. The only other item I took from that building is the sacred stone that lit my fire.

I now stay connected to the awakened Light within me. Just as you once reminded me, 'light out of darkness' is the meaning of my name. I hope that I am living up to it.

Your friend,

Claire des Tenebres

Sophia springs out of her seat and runs to Astar in celebration, "She's doing it Astar. Claire has kept her promise! She connects with her awakened Light, and in doing so she is lifting her spirit and the spirit of so many others along the way."

Sophia can't contain her joy. She runs outside, looks to the heavens, and calls out with gratitude. "The voices…they are being helped…it is really happening….the voices from the wilderness are finding their way to the Light as they help one another. It is true, we are all connected."

As she sits on the steps of the front porch, her gaze falls onto the one stepping stone that is missing its sacred symbol, the one that has eluded her for so long. Her elation returns to Earth once again.

Even though, time spreads the loving message from the heart of Hope's Haven to the four corners of the Earth, Sophia continues to wait patiently for Love to bring down the walls that separate us.

CHAPTER THIRTY-ONE

Astar nods to Roger, "Take a look." She points out the window toward the gravel drive. "Earnest is teaching Cody how to shift the gears in your old truck." It is the same truck in which Roger taught Sophia how to drive, upon her return home. The truck is spurting and stalling up the driveway as Earnest patiently explains the 'art of finessing the clutch' to Cody.

The bond of trust has forged the two of them together over the past ten years. Astar reflects upon their strong relationship as she smiles and exclaims, "Time is turning boys into men."

Roger admires their union. He remembers a conversation he had with Earnest, from many years ago. His heart is warmed as he reflects back on that candid exchange, when he conveyed the deep connection of love felt by two souls.

Roger stops to wonder silently, "How much longer must I wait before reuniting with my soul's mate?"

The Universe calms his anxious heart with the gift of images of Hope, hovering close by.

Roger then returns to the conversation with Astar, "Earnest and Cody, they were two young boys at heart, looking for someone to care for them. Then one day their souls connected, lifting each other up from the depths of their wounded lives. They now lean on each other with kindness, patience, trust and love. I couldn't imagine a stronger bond between another father and son. I'm proud of them for seeing the potential within each other, and themselves."

Sophia is expressing the same sentiment as she views Earnest and Cody from her bedroom deck. Long ago, she saw the future for the two. Love sparked between them when young Cody entrusted his tiny hand to Earnest's palm upon their first meeting. Their connection was instant, though the relationship took time to build. Together they found the meaning of unconditional love and the discovery that while any man can make a child, it takes a loving soul *to father* one.

CHAPTER THIRTY-TWO

The Universe hears our quietest thoughts…

In the depth of the night Sophia awakes. The scent of perfume is close. She arises from her sleeping state to follow the sweet fragrance. From the corner of her eye she sees the image of her angelic mother standing atop the staircase near her father's bedroom door. An iridescent tear falls from Hope's face as she floats into his room.

Sophia runs across the hall as her intuition silently conveys the hard truth. "This can't be happening!" Defiantly she calls out, "Dad, Dad, are you ok?" She bursts into his room to find him resting ever so peacefully in his bed. A memory book of times gone by with his beloved wife has fallen open upon his chest. In the clutches of his right hand is Hope's wedding ring, as if he is waiting to place it upon her finger once again.

Sophia runs to him in tears. "No! Daddy, no! Wake up Dad, wake up! Don't go!" She screams as she holds him tightly, rocking him back and forth. "Why are you leaving me? Not now Dad, not yet. I need you." Sophia loses herself in grief as the shock of his passing shoots through her heart.

The deep sorrow awakens Astar. She rushes into Roger's bedroom but suddenly stops at the vision she witnesses hovering right above the scene. The sweet scent of perfume is Hope. She has returned to meet Roger's soul at this time of his sacred passage.

Astar places her hand under Sophia's chin to lift her tear-filled gaze toward the beauty of Love that is surrounding them. Sophia sees the vision of her mother leading her father through the white light. Her father's words resonate through the stillness, "When our souls meet and unite, we uplift each other to a higher realm. I am with my beloved once again, Hope is by my side. Our darling Sophia, you have the Truth within your heart, share this Wisdom so all may unite as One."

Sophia watches as Love unites. Two beams of light become one and diffuse into the heavens. The room is surrounded by the electric magnetism of Love as the wheel of time continues to turn the cycles of life.

Astar, Cody and Earnest join Sophia throughout the night and into daybreak. They share the solemnness of Roger's passing by consoling, weeping and even laughing over the great times they've experienced with Roger.

Exhaustion pulls on Cody's eyelids as he fights to stay awake. Earnest also feels the heaviness of a sleepless night, but neither one is willing to leave Sophia's side.

Astar cradles Sophia in her arms throughout the night. When her tears become bitter at the sudden loss of her father, Astar sweetens them with a gentle embrace and loving memories of the times they shared.

CHAPTER THIRTY-THREE

The sun is awakening the gardens and meadows ever so slowly this morning as it blesses the mighty oak in preparation for Roger's ashes. The past few days have been a blur, while making the necessary arrangements, and consoling the grieving hearts of all who knew Roger.

People from near and far come to honor Roger's memory. It is a quiet service, but once everyone has gone, Sophia sits alone in silence, watching the rhythm of Nature. There is a continuous breeze, as if angels' wings are attempting to lift her thoughts and keep her focused on her path.

Sophia spends many days in the garden under the willow tree, in deep meditation. Her nights are passed under the blanket of stars that watch over us as we sleep. Many times, she reflects on the meaning of her own life. She questions the Universe: "How much longer will I be here? What must I do to fulfill my potential? When can I soar into the Celestial Heavens to be one with the Light?"

The Universe echoes the departing words of her dear father, "...you have the Truth within your heart, share this Wisdom so all may unite as One."

Slowly, Sophia begins to rise out of her sorrow. The angels' efforts finally take hold as her focus shifts toward her destined path.

One evening, she is compelled toward her sacred veil, once again. While kneeling on the stairs in front of her mystic veil, her hand graces its outer fringe, as a new vision expresses itself:

A beautiful patina of our blue-green globe appears. A single drop of blood falls and drips from north to south upon the disk.

Once the line is drawn the land divides, feuding faiths attack both sides. The blue-green disk turns black and white, hiding Truth from each other's sight.

The war is heightened. They no longer cope, with this divide that lost all hope. But a distant light finds hearts that heed. She shows the path for those who lead. The wheel must turn for wars to cease. A newborn child will forge this Peace.

The veil suddenly turns a solid midnight-blue and becomes still of all imagery.

Sophia desperately pleads, "Wait, what does this mean? There must be more!" She calls out to her Sages, for help in deciphering this message. There is no response. Sophia's ego begins to see an opportunity to rise up again. It feeds upon her growing impatience as she angrily calls out to the Universe, "How much longer must we wait for the wheels of time to turn!? How many *more* drops of blood must be shed before humanity finds courage, love...Truth?!!"

Her ego and spirit battle as the frustration builds. Sophia tears back her veil to reach the hidden passage behind her private library. She runs down the winding staircase into the garden where dawn is about to break through the darkened skies.

Sophia finds her way to her willow tree and sits beneath it. She breathes deeply, attempting to quiet the vile actions of her ego, as she reflects on the images upon her veil. The breeze calms the tensions in the air as it dances between the willow branches. Sophia allows her inner spirit to guide her once again.

The rising sun paints the landscape with a warm pink hue. A beautiful white dove flies to her side as Rose's voice fills Sophia's thoughts. "My darling Sophia, over the past years I have taught you all that I have and all that I am. You and I are one. Stay connected to your guiding Spirit of Love, and light the path for others. As they seek Truth, may they find Love." With those words, the dove flies off into the dawn of a new day.

With the rising sun, Rose's wise words guide Sophia along her mystic path. It has been her own fears that have held her back from reaching her true potential. Up until this moment, her thoughts were focused on the darkness, ignorance and destruction of the warring land. But now, she sees the Light...it is from this Light that courage, wisdom and creation will come.

Sophia feels her strong connection with the Spirit once again, as she unveils the wisdom, "The path for Peace is clear. It is the simplest deed of all!"

CHAPTER THIRTY-FOUR

Cody's favorite errand is to replenish the weekly supplies. This means he gets to drive the truck into town, all on his own. Each week he stops at the General Store to purchase the items on Astar's list and after loading up the truck, he walks back into the store.

He remembers the lost little boy, who used to pray for a loving home, at the wishing well. In a gesture of gratitude, he buys a single bar of chocolate with his earnings from small jobs he's completed for the neighbors and villagers. He walks out of the store and sits upon the wooden planks of the raised sidewalk, giving thanks to his angel, Sophia, for saving him.

Today, as he leans back against a post and slowly peels back the wrapper of his chocolate, he looks down Main Street toward the port. There, he spots a young couple that looks lost and scared--two emotions Cody remembers from his distant past.

He watches as the young man wipes away the tears from his companion's face, as he leans over to help her up from the bench. When she stands, Cody notices that she is pregnant…very pregnant.   Her steps are slow as she negotiates the cobble stones near the port.

Cody puts away his chocolate, jumps into the truck and drives down to the couple. "Excuse me. Can I give you a lift?" He startles the couple with his act of kindness. Their fear does not allow them to accept the offer. But Cody won't give up so easily. "Do you need help finding a place to stay?"

The young woman falters in her step. Cody jumps from the truck to help the couple. "Look, you can't just walk these streets in your condition. Let me help you."

The man finally speaks in desperation to help his young wife. "We have travelled far in search of a sanctuary. We have heard there is a place near this town, where help reaches out to those in need. Do you know of such a place? Does it truly exist?" His voice is filled with trepidation at the thought of hearing that their distant travels were based on a myth.

Cody opens the truck door and reaches toward the couple, inviting them to take a seat. "I know this place. I am heading there myself. You gotta let me help you. Your wife is in no shape to walk up this hill in her condition." Cody is afraid she might pop right then and there, due to all the stress and exertion of climbing the hill. "Besides, Hope's Haven is too far on foot with your luggage."

"Yes! That's it…a haven of hope is what we have heard." The young woman receives confirmation that they are on their destined path, as she gratefully accepts the ride.

After a short and quiet drive, Cody carefully pulls up the driveway at Hope's Haven. He parks as close to the garden gate as possible. With a toot of the horn, Earnest and Sophia arrive to assist with the supplies when they are surprised by the bounty of gifts Cody brings back with him.

Delighted by the arrival of guests, Sophia opens the truck door and extends a hand to help them out of the truck. The young man jumps out to assist his wife to the edge of the seat before she wiggles herself down to her feet. It is then that Sophia sees a beautiful shaft of white light grace the woman's belly. Sophia's joy and excitement overflow as she welcomes the new visitors. In her forethought is the connection between the brilliance of the light upon this unborn child, and the guidance of the images upon her sacred veil.

Sophia is smiling from ear to ear as she begins with introductions, "My name is Sophia. Welcome to Hope's Haven...welcome to the Sanctuary for Peace." She slowly walks across the stepping stones from the gate to the front door of the mansion, leading both guests along their path.

Upon reaching the porch steps, before entering the home, the young man replies, "Forgive me, Miss Sophia, my name is Sulayman and my beautiful wife is named Ruya. We have left our homeland in hopes that you can help us. Have we come to the right place?"

"Sulayman, Ruya, you've come to the right place. The Sanctuary for Peace is open to all seekers of Truth." She lays a hand on Sulayman's shoulder, while her other hand gently touches Ruya's belly. "You are all welcome to stay until your heart receives the guidance you seek." With those words Sophia feels a rush of energy, then the vision of families crying from a distant land, enter her mind. She begins to hear and see this young couple's story--who they are, and why they've come. Sophia welcomes their arrival as she sees the near future, just as the veil had revealed it.

"You must be exhausted from your long travels. Please come in, we'll have some tea and get you settled into a comfortable room." Sophia helps them into the kitchen as Cody and Earnest bring in the supplies.

Astar turns to see the young pregnant woman enter the kitchen. She exuberantly sings out to everyone, as if she's the town crier "Love is going bless us all with this child!" She gives Ruya a warm hug and pulls out a seat for her at the kitchen table. Astar looks knowingly at Sophia, "Well, we thought this time wound never come, but here you all are…and we are so happy to have you join us."

Sulayman and Ruya enjoy the warm greeting, and welcome a soothing cup of tea, as they sit around the table. Once the tea has calmed them down, Sulayman releases his hopes and fears to the kindness and love he feels around him. "I must tell you everything before we can rest here tonight, in your beautiful home."

Ruya gently squeezes his hand for support as she nervously bites her lip. She knows the Sanctuary for Peace is their last hope. They have nowhere else to turn, not now, not when she is due to have this child within a month.

Sulayman slowly begins, "It is true that we have travelled from a distant land. But we did not have the blessing of our families when we departed. You see, my wife and I are from two different sides of a dividing wall, in a nation that has only known war." He gently hugs his wife. "When I first saw Ruya, I knew that she is the one for me--my other half, my one true love."

Ruya softly adds, "It was instant for me too. But I knew my father would never allow this union. I can still hear his angered voice, 'I am the leader of this tribe. I cannot allow my daughter to marry the son of my enemy! He may one day lead his armies against me!' My father can be very forceful, even with his own family." Ruya's fear and disappoint appear as teardrops and roll from her rose-colored cheeks onto her belly.

Sulayman hugs her as he says, "It has not been easy. We tried to deny our love. Then we tried desperately to hide our relationship from our feuding tribes. But we could not betray our souls any longer; I willfully gave up my lineage to the leadership of this warring land. I am now just a man, who fell in love with the daughter of my father's enemy." He kisses Ruya's hand. Then he raises their united hands in defiance to the two opposing leaders, who would agree to only one thing in life, to have this marriage annulled at once. Sulayman restates, "I would give up everything to be with my one true love."

Ruya caresses her husband's face then continues, "We ran away from the hatred in our divided land to the mountains where the great Magi live. They are known to be the wisest men of our entire land. They sanctified our secret marriage in the hills then told us stories of a peaceful haven where hope lives."

Sophia smiles at the magnificent way the Universe connects us all. "...and here you are...everything is just as it should be. You may stay with us as long as you wish."

For the first time in over eight and half months of running and hiding from their angry fathers' reach, Sulayman and Ruya ease into their surroundings. Sophia's demeanor brings the peacefulness they long for in their new marriage. The calmness releases Ruya's tense hold upon the growing life within her round belly. The baby moves with joy and the sense of freedom soon to come.

CHAPTER THIRTY-FIVE

It's the first day of summer and Sophia awakes in the pre-dawn hours. She is eager to greet the sun as it comes to life. She quietly goes down her private stairway and walks around the rose garden toward the peaceful sway of her willow tree. When she passes the porch she is startled by the voice of another early riser.

"Good morning my gracious host. I hope I have not disturbed your sleep." Ruya is sitting back, rocking gently in one of the chairs upon the porch, looking past the garden gate to the meadow flowers. "I love to watch the morning light awaken all the colors of the day."

"Good morning Ruya. Not to worry, you have not disturbed my sleep. My rising hours are often spent in the gardens, giving thanks for the coming day, as well. But, shouldn't you be resting, for the little life growing inside of you?" Sophia asks, while smiling at the roundness of Ruya's belly.

Sophia senses something special within Ruya as she silently debates the evidence with herself, "Has Ruya been enlightened to the mystic wisdom? Ruya entrusted their marriage vows to the wisdom of the Magi. How could she have known of their hilltop home, unless she had been guided to them? Also, Ruya has been the force behind their distant travels to Hope's Haven, she follows her intuition."

It is all true! Ruya does envision a time of peace and unity within her divided land, and she can also see Sophia's deep connection with the Light that guides the path to Peace.

Sophia determines that she has a partner in Ruya, for they share the same vision—to awaken the Light of Love within each of us while resolving the darkness of fear amongst all of us.

As if on cue, Astar pokes her head out of the front door. "Tea anyone?" she whispers softly, so the others don't wake-up. Then she walks outside with a tray full of cups 'n' saucers and a pot of aromatic tea. Her every step is slow and steady, to quiet the rattle of the fragile butterfly-handled teacups.

The three ladies sit upon that porch, sipping tea and chatting as they await the wonders of the day. The sun warms the meadow flowers then slowly rises above the tree tops. The morning hours pass while the three women share in the divinity of Mother Nature...her creatures, her light, her wisdom and ultimately they connect with her Love.

A breeze captures Sophia's attention as it dances with tiny willow leaves upon the fourth stepping stone. It settles the leaves into a perfect symbol of unity as the sun embraces the mystic circle with a ray of Light.

Sophia's mind races at the possibilities held within today. The potential is present, of bringing together hearts and minds. Her intuition wisely tells her, "The potential is near to shift to Love from fear." Sophia then whispers, under her breath, "This is truly a mystical time." Both Astar and Ruya hear her message with crystal clarity.

Astar rests one hand on Ruya's belly, the other on Sophia's cheek, "My dears, each one of us carries the power of Love...today, this power will unite." Astar then shares a vision as it reveals itself. "Two pebbles have emboldened the stone wall of separation and hatred....once the pebbles are *moved*, the walls will come down."

Just then, the crunching sound of gravel beneath the weight of car tires signals the vision into action. First a white limousine and then a taxi pull up the driveway and stop. The man in the taxi gets out first and promptly makes his way toward the garden gate. Then the man from the limousine hurriedly exits his car and heads in the same direction. If their expressions were not so stern, it would be comical, the way the two of them attempt to outwalk each other's step.

Ruya flinches with tension and fear when she recognizes the two men. They proceed to unleash a barrage of unsavory words toward each other. The men cross paths toward the gate as they continue to bicker, yell and curse at each other; awakening everyone in the mansion.

The rage becomes explosive between the two men as they spew venomous words of hatred at each other. The heavens hear their dreadful noise and the summer skies fill with giant dark clouds that rumble and roar.

Just as the two men reach the gate; Earnest bursts through the front door and runs to them. He grabs a fistful of each man's collar and lifts them up so they can barely touch the ground with their toes. In a tremendous balance between hero and outlaw, Earnest calmly informs the men through his gritting teeth, "Keep your tempers in check! You are on sacred land, at a Sanctuary for *Peace*...and there are ladies present." He releases the two upon their acquiescence to Earnest's strong suggestion. Then he turns and opens the gate, "Now, won't you please come in?"

Once through the gate, the men stop suddenly. They have found what they have been chasing. Unexpectedly, the first man drops to his knees. His greatest fears are confirmed. He begins to cry, and pray and even beg, "My daughter, my only jewel, what have you done? Why did you not confide in me? How could you keep this hidden from your family?--You are with child!" Tears flow from his eyes turning his anger into shame as his body wilts to the ground with devotion and prayer for this new life. Ruya is his only child, and the only hope of producing an heir to the leadership of his divided land. He feels he has let his nation down by chasing Ruya away with his strong demands of obedience.

Ruya runs to her father's side, she too is moved to tears at the reunion with him, for she has missed him dearly. The nine months of running away, from her family and the life she knew, have taken their toll. She tries to lift her father up as she confesses, "I could not risk the outcome of losing my one true love. Father, father, tell me you understand. Tell me you forgive me."

The winds pick up and the rains begin as the second man looks down upon his opponent with contempt. He begins to charge forward in pursuit of his own son. His emboldened ego fuels his temper once again as he yells at Sulayman, "You are no son of mine! You have ruined the family name with this illegal marriage! Now you dare to bring this unlawful child under my name and our proud flag?!" He takes long, fast strides across the first three stepping stones then in a most humbling tumble he trips and falls over the fourth stone. Blood is gushing from his chin as he is overcome by shock and disgrace.

Sophia moves to help him, but Astar holds her back as she points to the ray of Light that is now shining upon Ruya's father, Akili. He stands and rushes to assist his fallen adversary, Chayim. Desperate to stop the bleeding, he takes a clean handkerchief from his pocket and holds it firmly over the gash. Chayim's blood seeps through and drips from the two men onto the earth.

Chayim looks upon the hand of his enemy as it holds the white cloth upon his chin. He watches a single drop of blood fall away from the chapped knuckles of Akili's hand and splatter upon the fourth disk as he surrenders his ego.

In Chayim's humble state, the Light can reach his heart from many directions. He looks at Akili--deep into his eyes. For the first time Chayim sees Akili as a man, a father and his equal instead of his enemy. The two men become aware of the other's presence, his right to exist, his will to excel, his fears of failure, and even his love for the people of his land. Both their hearts were opened in this one single moment of time.

Sophia approaches them and helps to lift them to their feet. She joins her hands with the blood-stained hands of the two leaders. They feel her aura surround them as she guides them to Ruya and Sulayman, who are steadfastly at each other's side. Sophia looks into Ruya's eyes and secretly asks for her trust, as she lays the hands of the two men upon Ruya's pregnant belly. The baby moves under the pressure. Both men recoil their hands from the light of Love that sparks from within Ruya's womb.

Sophia begins to turn her nightmares of the past into dreams of the future as she speaks to the leaders of a torn land. "In times gone by, fear found fertile ground to grow the seed of hatred into a massive wall of separation that divides one land and its weary people. The years of hatred allowed fear to bring darkness, ignorance and destruction upon this land."

Once again, Sophia leads their bloody hands back to Ruya's beautiful round belly. She lets the wisdom of her intuition speak for her, "Feel the life that tumbles and rolls beneath your palms. The blood that courses through this child is the union of your bloodlines. It is the union of two lives in Love. You can choose to unite your land and its people...now, with one united intention. It's the simplest deed of all. All you have to do is...Choose Love!"

In that moment, Ruya lets out a scream that announces the baby is on the way. The tension and excitement have brought on her labor pains. Sulayman takes her into his arms and carries her to a bed where she can gain a little comfort, as Astar and Sophia scramble to help Ruya prepare herself for the birth of this child.

The men pace back and forth, outside the bedroom door for hours. Each leader is pondering Sophia's last words, 'all you have to do is, choose Love'.

Upon the dawn of a new day, the joyous cry of a newborn baby resounds from the Sanctuary. Sulayman walks out of the bedroom, carrying his newborn babe. He walks toward the leaders of the divided land and solemnly says, "Our dark history is stained by the blood of death." He lifts the baby toward the two men then pleads, "If you choose to hold this child within your hands, then our future will unite by the blood of Life, and bring Peace upon our divided land."

Both men are drawn to this child of Love as they lay their hands upon the bundle of joy. Then Chayim takes the child into his arms tenderly, as Akili holds its tiny hand in his palm. They look back into the bedroom where Ruya is surrounded by a peaceful glow. They carry the child to his mother, and both men step to the same side of the bed. They look at themselves and each of the people around them--frail ones, bold ones, "perfect" ones...some with imperfection right out front others with their flaws hidden deep within.

They imagine that this miracle of life could not have happened, if any one of them had not done their part. Chayim reflects on the Love that shines from each soul around him. He states, "We are all connected in this life. We are one in the eyes of God."

Akili reaches over and clutches Chayim's shoulder, "The path is clear for us now." They both respond with the awakened Light within their hearts, "We choose Love."

CHAPTER THIRTY-SIX

An explosion of fall colors, paints the landscape around the Sanctuary. Sophia leans against her willow tree viewing the sacred symbols that have graced her path. As her view reaches the missing symbol of unity, she reflects on her distant visitors.

It has been three months since Sulayman and Ruya awakened the Light of Love in the heart of their nation's leaders. The moment still resonates within Sophia's heart, when Chayim and Akili uttered their intention, "We choose Love."

Often times Sophia wonders how things are progressing between the two leaders and their people since returning to their nation. Her thoughts continue to stoke the eternal flame as it guides the path to Love. Her pensive day-dreams are awakened by the sound of the old truck as it grumbles up the driveway.

She hears it struggle up the hill as Cody drives up the long gravel road. He is returning from an errand. The port had called about a package at the docks that needed to be picked up. Cody pulls up to the gate and parks. He lifts the large package from the bed of the truck and carries the heavy bundle through the garden gate a few feet, where he puts it down to rest.

Sophia walks over and curiously asks, "What do you have here, Cody?" She turns the bulky package to see it is addressed to 'HOPE'S HAVEN, A Sanctuary for Peace' with nothing else written on the box.

"Cody, help me open this, will you?" Sophia's intuition is fueling her anticipation as she wonders quietly, "Could this package contain the news I've been hoping for?"

Cody eagerly yells out, "Astar, Earnest, come here, we have a package!"

They all have a hand in freeing the contents as they rip away the wrapping to reveal a magnificent stone disk. Earnest and Cody wonder why someone would ship a rock clear across the world while Astar and Sophia smile over the possibilities held within the wonderful symbol that has been carved into the rare stone.

"There's a note." Cody says, pulling it out from between the wrappings, and handing it to Sophia. She slides the note from its envelope as she reads:

To our most gracious host, Sophia and her Sanctuary for Peace:

We choose Love. That is our promise!

We are following the path that you have shown us. Upon returning to our land we began the process of uniting the tribes under one nation. Our newborn grandchild is the witness to this promise that we shall forever protect.

As the first step, we crushed the stone walls that separate us. We now use the stones to rebuild our schools and homes and pave the way to a brighter future. It is amazing what can

be done once one walks out of the shadows of fear and into
the bright light of Love.

We are sending to you the cornerstone of this ancient wall
as a mark of our promise. The leadership of our united land
has individually and willfully forged their stamp of honor onto
this stone. Each stamp links with the stamp before and after
it, encircling this stone and forming a circle of unity. May
this stone find a peaceful home within your graceful gardens.

Miss Sophia, you showed us that Love will come for all
who choose it. You are a beacon of Light for our vision,
intention and peace. This guiding Light is in the thoughts,
words and actions of our people as we maintain the promise
to "Choose Love".

In eternal gratitude,

Chayim, Akili, Sulayman and Ruya

Sophia kneels by the place-holder stepping stone as she
clears the path for her missing symbol. She is overwhelmed,
by receiving this symbol of unity and the promise for Peace,
as her tears of joy fall upon the stone. Astar, Earnest and
Cody join Sophia. They place the gift in its rightful place--
along the path, from the garden gate to the heart of the home,
at the Sanctuary for Peace.

CHAPTER THIRTY-SEVEN

The wheels of time keep turning as the years come and go. A resident docent quietly welcomes visitors to the Sanctuary for Peace. The library walls are covered with notes and letters from seekers who have found their guiding Light over the many decades that have now passed.

Off in the distance, Sophia wanders deep into the wilderness of Hope's Haven, where she comes upon Mirror Pond. She walks along the banks of the glassy water, without noticing the reflection of her trusted friend, the timber wolf, at her side.

A weeping willow sways in the breeze as it offers Sophia a quiet resting place. She reposes against the tree as her long gray hair falls around her shoulders softly. She dips her fingers into the soothing pond water and fondly reflects on the moments of her life as the wolf gently tugs at her shirt tail. Her most cherished companion has come back to lead Sophia along her journey to the Light, where Rose and Astar await with all the other loved ones that have passed before us.

The celestial skies welcome Sophia home as her Wisdom reflects upon Earth. Sophia's translucent light forever shines for us. Upon every ray of sunshine, her promise can still be heard, "Seek Truth and you will find your potential!"

The voice of a distant sage whispers upon the winds of the Universe, "May we all reach our full potential...to *'choose Love'* in all our thoughts, words and actions."

CHAPTER THIRTY-EIGHT

The night of time has come, as she lays the strand of pearls back onto the midnight-blue velvet. She leans back comfortably as she acknowledges the beauty of Nature's creation. Then, with one final breath, she sleeps…until it is time to awaken, once again.

ABOUT THE AUTHOR

KATY TACKES

Katy was born in Persia to a celebrated furniture designer. At a very young age she immigrated to Canada, where her immense love and gratitude for Mother Nature blossomed.

She has been gifted the opportunity of living in Paris, France, and traveling throughout Europe, Asia, New Zealand, the Middle-East and North America, reinforcing her belief that "we are all connected…we are One".

It is through her love and studies of theosophy and ancient wisdom that she continues her quest for Truth.

Get the EACH TIME SHE WAKES
companion writing journal

GOD CREATED YOU TO SEE WHAT YOU WOULD
SHOW HIM

Forward by Katy Tackes

22345845R00123

Made in the USA
Middletown, DE
27 July 2015